MARGARET OF MOLOKAI

MARGARET OF MOLOKAI

MEL WHITE

WORD BOOKS
PUBLISHER
WACO, TEXAS

MARGARET OF MOLOKAI
Copyright © 1981 by Mel White

The Scripture quotation on page 105 is from the American Standard Version, copyright © 1901, published by Thomas Nelson & Sons.

Scripture quotations identified NIV are from the Holy Bible: New International Version. Copyright © 1978 by the New York International Bible Society.

ISBN –0–8499–0294–0
Library of Congress catalog card number: 81–51007
Printed in the United States of America

To

Sarah Bunker
Bessie Clinton
Mary Jolenta
Alice Kahokuoluna
Jackie Wiggins
and the other great women in Margaret's life

and to
Grandma Ruth Rear
one of the great women in mine

Now on his way to Jerusalem, Jesus traveled along the border between Samaria and Galilee. As he was going into a village, ten men who had leprosy met him. They stood at a distance and called out in a loud voice, "Jesus, Master, have pity on us!"

When he saw them, he said, "Go, show yourselves to the priests." And as they went, they were cleansed.

One of them, when he saw he was healed, came back, praising God in a loud voice. He threw himself at Jesus' feet and thanked him—and he was a Samaritan.

Jesus asked, "Were not all ten cleansed? Where are the other nine? Was no one found to return and give praise to God except this foreigner?" Then he said to him, "Rise and go; your faith has made you well."

LUKE 17:11–19, NIV

CONTENTS

9

A PREVIEW

The tropical sun rose lazily over Diamond Head, streaking
Pearl Harbor with gold. But from her perch in a plumeria
tree high above the sidewalks of Moiliili, Margaret, a
twelve-year-old Hawaiian girl, hardly noticed this light
show. Already her palm basket overflowed with the white
and yellow blossoms she would wear that day before the
royal court. Margaret had been chosen from her neighborhood to perform the ancient hula for the 1934 May Queen
on the capitol steps in Honolulu. She was poor, virtually
uneducated and decidedly underprivileged, a needy child
from the slums of the spreading city. But every day, even
when she felt tired or hungry or ill, Margaret practiced the
hula, an ancient Polynesian dance, with its intricate
movements of hands and hips. Her lithe body draped in ti
leaves, coarse cloth and plumeria, Margaret dreamed that
one day she would dance her way into a new and better
life.

On that first day in May, nearly fifty years ago,
Margaret's dream collapsed forever. As she rushed from
the stage, her face flushed by the applause of the admiring
crowd, a tall, thin man reached out a bony hand, grasped
her arm and steered her away from the other dancers. For
one frightening moment, she stood staring up at him under
the banyan tree on King Street. She recognized him

vaguely as Mr. Kikila, the health inspector who occasionally patrolled their neighborhood to the hoots and jeers of all her neighbors. Still, Margaret had no idea of the horror in the news he brought that day.

"You are a leper, child, and you will come with me."

There was no time for tears. Since January 3, 1865, when the Hawaiian Legislature passed a law entitled "An Act to Prevent the Spread of Leprosy," suspected victims were quickly taken to the Receiving Station at Kalihi, isolated from family and friends, positively diagnosed and eventually sent to Kalaupapa, the leprosy settlement on Molokai. On that lonely isle, for thirty-three years, Margaret watched her own body scar and shrink from the disease. There her twenty-two-year-old sister, another patient, died in the pounding surf. There, over the decades, Margaret watched her three afflicted husbands die. There her newborn children were taken from her arms and shipped to foster homes on Oahu. There she dressed the sores of the living and closed the eyes of the dying, deformed victims of a disease the ancient Egyptians called "death before death." Then in 1969, her leprosy arrested at long last, Margaret was released from Molokai.

Margaret's story must be told, for it reaches each of us who has ever prayed for a miracle but not received the miracle we prayed for. Today, Margaret lives and works in the Oahu Towers Project, a high-rise slum on the edge of Honolulu. Her life is ending as it began, surrounded by poverty, hopelessness and horror. She is sixty years old. She is still poor and underprivileged. Her once lovely body is permanently disfigured by the disease. On the bureau in her tiny, one-room apartment, there is a gray and fading picture of a young Hawaiian dancer, holding a pet white rabbit. Her story is the fascinating account of one dream that died and of another that took its place.

I watched Margaret walk on damaged feet to visit the lonely, the sick and the imprisoned in that high-rise nightmare where she lives. I watched her reach out withered hands to give away clothing, food and money to neighbors in need. God may not have given Margaret the miracle she wanted. But He gave her another kind of miracle. His Spirit is present and working in her life. In spite of every possible handicap, she is full of hope and purpose and joy. These are the modern-day miracles. At this moment in time, when we who seem to have so much can offer our world so little, it both shames and inspires us to look at Margaret, who seems to have so little but offers the world so much.

That May Day so long ago, Margaret thought she would never dance again, but just last year, before a tear-blinded congregation of her fellow worshipers at Kalihi Union Church, she raised her hands and danced, as the psalmist David commanded, her own sweet dance of praise. There is something in the works and words of Margaret that will help us all want to dance that dance ourselves.

MEL WHITE
Honolulu, Hawaii
January, 1981

I.

APARTMENT
IN
MOILIILI

1922–34

Kona winds flattened breakers and blew white sea foam across the deserted Honolulu beaches onto the flooded streets of Waikiki. Tourists sipped room-service mai tais and watched palm trees twist in the gale. The tropical rain squall had traveled up Kalakaua Avenue from Diamond Head to Beretania with such blinding force that drivers abandoned cars and shoppers ran inside the nearest building for cover.

Charles Simon Carl Frederick stood in the doorway of Kekaulike's fishmarket, glad for once that he still wore the red wool jacket of the Royal Prussian Marching Band. The burnished brass buttons were ten years missing and the gold braid on each shoulder had long since torn away, but he was warm and dry against the storm as was the hidden infant he cradled against his chest.

Blinking back the rain, the young German musician looked up King Street in the direction from which Moriah and William would come, then down into the face of his latest child, Margaret. *Hānai*, an old Polynesian custom allowing parents already overblessed with offspring to give the extra child away, was barbaric when judged by the mores of his European past. But *hānai* was necessary if he and Edith and the other children were to survive the depression in Paradise. It was legal and moral and really

17

rather commonplace in the islands, but the young father, still in his early thirties, found it difficult to imagine handing this brown-eyed child of his own flesh and blood into the hands of his wife's sister, Moriah, and her boyfriend, William Kaupuni.

Trapped by the storm and given unwelcome moments for brooding, Charles wondered how, in only ten years, Paradise had become a nightmare. He still remembered clearly that first day in the islands when the German ocean liner from Hamburg docked in Honolulu Harbor and he and seventy other soldier-musicians walked wide-eyed past the Aloha Tower into the waiting plumeria leis and bare, outstretched arms of Hawaii. He remembered the embarrassed grins and good-natured gestures he and his buddies shared as those beautiful, brown-skinned girls danced their welcome. He remembered the Iolani Palace and the band concert they played with the Royal Hawaiians near the old Coronation stand.

In only one day, the beauty of the island and especially of the island women threatened to overwhelm this tuba-playing tourist from Westphalia. Then Charles met Edith, a local island girl whose ethnic roots stretched from the shores of China to the craggy cliffs of Ireland. One look at that Eurasian beauty with her laughing eyes convinced the soldier guest that he could wave good-bye to his Germanic past and live out his future in Hawaii.

At first it was easy to find work as a hotel musician. Then, with the growing depression, tourism dwindled. Employment dried up. Factory work was possible, but with each bad harvest or unseasonal storm came new unemployment. Families moved together into Honolulu slums. Wood frame houses with corrugated metal roofs soon were crammed with too many children and too little food. A person had to be practical to survive; and so, ten years after that first island welcome, Charles Frederick stood in the doorway of Kekaulike's fishmarket preparing to give his baby daughter to a near stranger.

The child awoke and began to cry. Moriah was late.
Margaret was hungry. Her father whispered to her in
German-accented pidgin English and rocked her gently up
and down. The rain stopped as suddenly as it had begun.
The tropical sun burned all remnants of the storm away.
White clouds undulated through brilliant blue skies, and
the foothills glistened emerald green. A rainbow joined the
Palolo Valley to the Ala Wai Canal. Then, the teenage girl,
Moriah, and her common-law husband, William Kaupuni,
stood before him. Quickly, Charles Frederick took the
crying child from his tattered scarlet tunic and gave
Margaret away forever.

That stormy day in November 1922 was not the last time
Margaret would be given away, locked out, abandoned or
even left alone to die. That she survived her first dozen
years of life was, in her own words, "some kin' miracle."
When she was only two or three years old, her adoptive
mother, Moriah—tired of motherhood and housewifery—
ran away with a young Filipino lover, leaving William with
the infant girl he had never really wanted. Months later,
he discovered Moriah had eloped and moved to Manila. To
keep his job and raise a child was no easy task.

William Kaupuni was a machinist apprentice at the
Honolulu Iron Works on the outskirts of that rapidly
sprawling city. He arrived every morning at sunrise just
as the hearth had been repaired and the tap holes of the
huge furnaces had been plugged. In the dingy locker room
in a cement building near the furnace, William put on
goggles and safety clothing provided by the plant to
protect him against the intense light, heat and sparks from
the molten metal. By 7:00 A.M., he entered the furnace
area, climbed the slippery metal ladder to his place behind
the driver of the charging machine and waited for the
melting bell.

Huge electromagnetic cranes lifted scrap iron and steel

into shredding machines. The shredded scrap was pressed into compact bales by hydraulic pressing machines. Other cranes lifted the bales into the charger. William Kaupuni helped control the charger that dumped the scrap into the open hearth furnace where it was melted by 3000-degree heat into molten metal and ladled into heavy ingot molds.

The noise was deafening. The white-hot heat intense. Sweat poured nonstop down his face and ran in rivulets down his back. His body ached. During the all-too-infrequent breaks, while his fellow employees reached for a can of Primo or lit up a hand-rolled cigarette, William sprinted for the parking lot.

For almost nine months, unknown to his employers, William used the back seat of a friend's car for Margaret's playpen and mobile day-care center. Each morning William would pack fruit, meat and rice into a metal lunch box and Margaret and her rag doll into a large wicker basket. When the break whistle sounded, William left the furnace area, fed, watered and walked his little daughter, locked her in again and returned to work. Margaret remembers those days with a simple, "I no bother. I understand. He would come, my father and the other one that own the car. They would check on me. I fine. Every day going work with my dad. Not bad, you know. At least we together. More than kids now."

William met Margaret's third mother at a cafe near the Iron Works. Ida moved into William's room just off South King Street in Moiliili when Margaret was five or six years old. The depression was in full force. Besides measles, venereal disease and leprosy, the *haoles* [foreigners] brought economic illness to the islands. Lines formed early in the day with those waiting for the injured fruit at the packing plant, for old bread at the bakeries and for the fish trimmings from Kekaulike's Market.

Ida worked as crate doctor on the night shift in Dole's

huge pineapple plant. As the still green fruit was crated for shipment from the Hawaiian Territory to the United States mainland, Ida would check each crate for broken slats and injured or over-ripe fruit. When a crate needed repair, she would hoist it from the moving belt, pry it open with the claw end of a hammer, replace the fruit or slat, then lift the crate back into place on the line.

The workers were paid for the amount of pineapple that was crated and prepared for shipment every day. Because they were paid by the crate or piece—thus "piece work"— everyone worked tirelessly between the opening and closing bells. Ida spent eight hours lifting and operating on forty-pound crates. If the belt slowed or the crates pyramided and collapsed on the workers, she would be blamed. She returned to their little apartment by 5:00 A.M. and dropped into restless sleep. William fixed his daughter breakfast and left her in the hands of the sleeping Ida.

William anesthetized his pain by consuming great quantities of cheap island beer or a "bathtub" brew they made at home with grape juice fermented in a pan by the natural yeast in a rotting Irish potato. "One bowl dat stuff and you mean drunk," Margaret remembers.

"When my dad drunk he beat my mother up. He beat her bad. She used to run with me. Take me. We hide in the bushes. You know, my dad, he was one big man. Then, my mother used to beat me after.

"Friends, Japanese neighbors, used to tell him, 'Oh, Kaupuni, your daughter had dirty licking today.'

"But when he ask me, I won't tell. I said, 'Nah.'

"He say, 'You sure, baby?'

"I say, 'Sure.' Because if tell going get licking next day.

"But he nevah believe me. One day he fooled my mother. He wasn't feeling well. So nevah tell her nothing. Came home early. I was in the corner, with no clothes on. She was beating me. She was beating me so hard I make *shishi* on floor. My father grab the strap. He say, 'Now I believe friends. Why you lick Margaret?' My mother nevah say nothing. He beat her once, then stop. Ida cry. My father cry. We all cry then."

Sunday morning was a very different trauma for the Kaupuni family. As the sun rose over the Maunalani Heights and streamed in through their torn screen porch, something mysterious happened to that same Ida who could outcurse any sailor in a Pearl Harbor dive and outwork any man at Hawaiian Pineapple.

Ida stood looking into the cracked mirror over the sink in the hallway that doubled as a kitchen and a washroom. As she pulled a plastic comb through her long brown hair, she sang quietly to herself, *"Jesu no ke Kahuhipa* [Saviour, like a shepherd, lead us]." Margaret lay on her floor pallet nearby and listened. William groaned, knowing well the battle that lay ahead—a battle he would lose, as he had lost Sunday after Sunday in the on-going war with Ida and her determination to have her family in church on the Lord's Day morning. The babies, Robert and Pilahi, were still asleep.

In the two years since Ida moved in with William, the family had grown by two members. Ida looked down at the sleeping infants. Pilahi had been another *hānai* baby, given to William and Ida by a distant relative who could not keep the child. Robert's arrival was even less expected. Ida had heard an infant crying somewhere in the pile of cardboard boxes and wooden packing crates in an alleyway behind a large vegetable market. She and Margaret searched until they found him wrapped in newspapers in the trash can where he had been abandoned. Without a word, Ida took the child home, bathed, dressed and named him. Ida still smiled to herself when she remembered William's surprised look the day she presented him with his first and only son.

Ida wakened Robert with a gentle shake, *"Aloha kakahiaka* [good morning]." Then she lifted Pilahi from the blanket and handed her to Margaret to change and dress.

"Put on *Lāpule lole* [Sunday clothes], Margaret. Time we go *kula Kāpaki* [Sunday school]." The children were Margaret's responsibility. By the time she was seven, Margaret was their nurse, housekeeper and nanny while Ida and William worked, fought and struggled to survive.

Ida had trained Margaret in household chores the year of Ida's sickness. For almost twelve months, Ida lay helpless in her bed, nearly paralyzed from a back injury sustained at Hawaiian Pineapple. Just as Margaret turned eight, she learned at the foot of her mother's bed how to wash and iron the clothing, to mix and strain the poi, to clean and fry the fish. Margaret went to the first grade but never returned to school because Ida needed her to take care of the children, to prepare the meals for the family and to clean their little apartment.

But Sunday school was different to Ida, more important than any other event in the week. She sat beside William on the bed and mussed his hair playfully with her hand.

"We no *hakakā* [fight] today. You come *hale pule* [church], no trouble. I fix you good *opihi* afta."

Groaning awake, still hungover from his Saturday-night bout with the "bathtub" brew, bribed with an offering of his favorite sea urchin chowder, William Kaupuni found it difficult to comprehend how every Sunday morning his siren became a saint. But he found it even more difficult, if not dangerous, to resist. If loving bribery didn't work, Ida was known to scold, rage, even beat him from the bed and out the door. He knew that on that one day when they all might sleep in, Ida would lead them in her proud procession across Honolulu, up the steps of the old Kawaiahao Church and into her favorite pew—or die trying.

William rose from his bed, splashed cold water onto his face and helped Margaret dress the children in the clothes Ida and Margaret had washed, patched, and ironed the day before. Margaret remembers as the family walked towards Kapiolani Street to board the number three bus to

Punchbowl that the neighbors whispered, "Those Kaupuni children always look so good on Sunday." Ida led the parade, holding Margaret's hand and looking back over her shoulder to see that Robert was not dawdling to play en route and that William, carrying Pilahi, wouldn't sneak out of line altogether.

As they disembarked the bus and proceeded down Punchbowl to King Street, the children could hear the congregation singing the opening praise:

> *Hoonani i ka Makua mau*
> *Ke Keiki me ka Uhane no.*
> *Ke Akua mau—hoomaikai pu*
> *Ko keia ao, ko kela ao.*

One hundred and ten years before, in 1820, a Christian missionary, the Reverend Hiram Bingham, dedicated his first church on that spot. By 1825, eight Hawaiian chiefs had been baptized there, and the people flocked to attend the overflow services in the open air. The High Chief Kalanimoku built a temporary *lānai* of native timbers and the Queen Regent Kaahumanu had a great hau tree planted under which she sat to worship. Five thousand people joined her under the sun on their straw mats and sang together Reverend Bingham's translation of the doxology into native Hawaiian. Translated back into English, it reads:

> Be Thou, O God, exalted high;
> And, as Thy glory fills the sky,
> So let it be on earth display'd,
> Till Thou art here as there obey'd.

Ida led her family up the steps of the Kawaiahao Church. She loved and revered the old church building, built by King Kamehameha's decree over a seven-year period from 1835 until 1842. She liked to run the children's hands over the rough, coral blocks cut from the sea by divers working with blunt axes in ten to twenty feet of water. She showed them how seabirds still picked at the tiny crevices in the building's stones for long-dead plant and fish life buried there. She pointed up at the huge wooden beams and told the children how each was cut and formed in the forests just north of their apartment in Moiliili. In the basement, after Hawaiian Bible Study, Ida showed Margaret the huge cornerstone made from Waianae sandstone and floated to Honolulu on a giant raft made from canoes and bamboo poles. The Kawaiahao Church was paid for by the king and erected by the people. Kawaiahao's second pastor, the Reverend R. Armstrong, said, "This church was a greater work for the Hawaiian people than Solomon's temple was for him."

Ida opened the Hawaiian hymnbook and handed it to her children. Margaret remembers her two favorite hymns were "Nearer My God to Thee" and "Saviour, Like a Shepherd, Lead Us." These two hymns, like much of imported Hawaiian hymnody, were translated by the lyric poet and missionary, the Reverend Lorenzo Lyons of Waimea, Hawaii. The Hawaiian people called him *Ka Haku Mele o ka Aina Mauna*, "Song-maker of the Mountain Land." Ida loved to sing. She hoped her children would inherit the musical and poetic gifts native to so many Hawaiians. As they sang that day the imported hymn tunes of Bach and Wesley and the native hymn tunes bearing such names as Maui, Wailoi and Punahou, their voices joined with the echo of a thousand Hawaiian workers who had sledded coral blocks, 14,000 hand-carved stones, and 100,000 handmade shingles across the landscape to this site while chanting songs of praise.

When the offering was taken, Ida opened her Hawaiian Bible and amazed William with the amount of cash she had stored away for the occasion. She shared it with her children to place it in the calabash as it was passed. When Robert whispered, Ida pointed to the *E Hāmau* [Be Quiet] signs posted on the handcarved stone pillars. And when the *kahuna pule*, the Reverend Aiko Akana, removed his shoes, walked in bare feet past the giant candlesticks and up the stairs to the pulpit and spoke eloquently of God's love, of Jesus' life, death and resurrection and of the powerful presence of the Holy Spirit, there was a hush only disturbed by the occasional snore of poor William or another forced parishioner still battling the effects of Saturday's late-night revelries.

When the final benediction was pronounced, Ida led her family down the stairs, onto the number seven bus back down Kapiolani Street and up the walk into their apartment in Moiliili for their lunch of rice and *opihi* chowder. On Sunday, something happened to Ida in the church when the people gathered to sing and pray and hear God's Word proclaimed; and she was desperate to pass it on to her children. They could tell by the way she watched them when they sat beside her in the pew or by the way she scolded them if they whispered or dozed in the service. At home, she taught them hymns and psalms by memory. She made them keep a little money in her Hawaiian Bible for their own offerings. Even in her most violent moments, exhausted by the endless hopelessness of her own life, or drunk and sick from her attempts to escape it, Ida tried to teach her children.

After one beating when Ida left her bruised and bloody, Margaret remembers moaning, "O, God, please take me away." Ida beat her again saying, "God give you life. God take away when he ready." Margaret was nine years old. She hated Ida then. But those childhood memories are softened now, for Margaret has survived the horror of her own life due, at least in part, to truths planted in her heart by Ida years long past. "I think my mother, even though she beat me, loved me. She knew what was right even though she could not do. And I think she wanted to give those things to me. So she passed them the only way she knew, poor thing. At least she tried, ya?"

Ida was determined that Margaret learn about God first, and learn to hula second. On her eighth birthday, she led her daughter by the hand to the old wood frame house of Margaret's Auntie Keaka, the neighborhood *kumu hula* or hula instructor. Ida knocked softly on the door.

Inside, a loud voice counted to four over and over again. The counting was interrupted occasionally by a loud, "Not dat way, dis way," and a slap of the coconut frond of a Niihau broom on some poor, unsuspecting foot or hip. Margaret heard the muffled cries of pain from inside and wanted to flee, but Ida held her hand all the tighter.

"Auntie?" Ida called gently.

Inside, the counting stopped and auntie called back still in ¼ time, "Go 'way, Ida. She too young. Bones too soft. Already tell you!"

"Margaret eight today, auntie. You say eight old enough."

Margaret could picture her auntie fanning herself with the palm fan and walking slowly to the door. The door opened. Auntie reached for Margaret's arm.

"O.K., Margaret. Come in. Good-bye, Ida."

The door slammed. Inside the old house, six girls, all older than Margaret, sat or lay around the room in various stages of exhaustion. Auntie put her hands on her wide, hula hips, wrinkled up her broad, craggy face, put back her head and laughed.

"Look at dem, Margaret. You want to hula? Look at dem."

Margaret looked down at the older girls fanning themselves and groaning softly, then up to her auntie. The little girl might have answered, "No"; but her auntie had swept across the room, lifting each girl lovingly but firmly to her feet.

"We show Margaret da hula. Won't we, girls? Da *Hula Ku'i Moloka'i.*"

At the name of the punch hula of Molokai, an ancient fast dance with stamping, heel twisting, thigh slapping, dipping of knees, doubling of fists and vigorous pretending to pull nets and spear fish, the girls groaned the louder.

Auntie picked up her Niihau broom and the groaning

stopped. Then, without any musical accompaniment, on some invisible signal from their *kumu hula*, the girls began to dance. Margaret stood in awe as they whirled about her closer and closer, until in unison they chanted, *A la'a ko ku i ke a'u* [now you are jabbed by the swordfish]" and danced toward her, taunting. Margaret jumped back as the dance ended, and the girls joined in auntie's laughter. Seeing her tremble, auntie lifted Margaret and carried her from the room.

"You will start tomorrow, Makalika, with one class of girls your own age. Now go tell Ida you need one skirt before you dance and sandals and one red top like da other girls. Run, child. Tomorrow you dance."

Margaret ran to Ida.

"I no like go. I learn hula by myself. You teach."

But Ida wouldn't listen and that next day the lessons began. Margaret remembers those twice-weekly sessions from 7:00 to 9:00 P.M. with mixed emotions.

"She no like shoulders move. So she test us with small jigga of water. Put on our shoulder. If that stayed, you all right. If it went down, even one drop, you get licking until you make 'em no fall. She was big lady, heavy, you know? And she used to kneel on our knees to break in and soften. She say, 'You girls young, soft, flexible. You bend while still can. I bend no more.' Then she laugh and stand on our feet until we cry from hurt.

"When I go home my mother had hot, hot wata with Hawaiian salt to drink fo'a take away the pain. I complain. Sometimes cry. But she not bad, auntie. She love the dance and she teach good. I learn good. It hurt, but I learn good; and when I went dance at Honolulu Hale before the May Queen, the people stand and clap, and I feel proud, you know, that I was that good."

The tour bus from Honolulu swayed dangerously close to the steep cliffs off the Pali Highway. Ladies from Wichita and Sheboygan in brightly patterned muumuus gasped and giggled while their husbands, in matching aloha shirts, clutched Brownie box cameras, snapped the passing scenery and teased their women with growing delight. Margaret and William were the only two locals on board this *haole* express. It was Margaret's twelfth birthday and, under pressure from Ida and his child, her father granted the gift she requested, a visit to the scenic Nuuanu Lookout in the mountains of the Koolau Range north and west of Honolulu.

Margaret, breathless with excitement as they reached the crest, left the bus and walked hand in hand with William toward the lookout point. Her father had been strangely quiet on the journey. She had to beg him to tell the stories of Kamehameha the Great, who forced the defeated warriors from Oahu to jump from the highest precipice when he conquered the island in 1795. He bought her ice cream from a vending truck; and when the cone was eaten, Margaret stole a piece of ice to chew from the chipped ice dripping in the afternoon sun.

The sky was sea blue. Playful white clouds boiled up over the fluted cliffs of the Ahuimanu Valley. The jungle colors ranged from light yellow to darkest green. They walked together beneath the vines all tangled in gaint hau trees. Margaret picked a yellow blossom and stuck it jauntily above one ear in her straight brown hair.

They were sitting in silence, looking down at the towns and pastures between the *pali* [mountain] and Kaneohe Bay, when William spoke.

"Your sister, Leilani, very sick."

Margaret had eleven brothers and sisters from her first set of parents, Edith and Charles Frederick. Through Ida and William, she had gained siblings twelve and thirteen, Robert and Pilahi. Leilani was the oldest and favorite child of her original parents, her natural mother's namesake.

"What *ma'i* [sickness] she have?" Margaret asked, still licking the melting ice.

Her father turned away and looked down the *pali*. For a long time he couldn't say the name.

"*Ma'i-Pākē*," he finally whispered.

Margaret was silent. She knew nothing of leprosy—neither the Hawaiian name, meaning "Chinese sickness" or the Latin *lepra*, meaning "scaly" from the lumps on the skin often caused by the disease. She was only twelve years old but she sensed her father's anguish and was frightened by it.

William explained to Margaret what would happen to her sister Leilani if the authorities discovered her sickness. Since January 3, 1865, when the Hawaiian Legislature passed a law entitled, "An Act to Prevent the Spread of Leprosy," suspected victims of the disease were hunted by representatives of the Board of Health, quickly taken to the Receiving Station at Kalihi, isolated from family and friends, positively diagnosed and eventually sent to Kalaupapa, the leprosy settlement on Molokai.

As they walked along the *pali*, he told her of the disease that began with a loss of feeling and ended with claw hands on its victims and—as he incorrectly understood—eventually ate away and disfigured the entire body. He told her about Molokai and the living dead who peopled the colony there. He told her, too, of a famous Hawaiian from the island of Kauai who refused to go to Molokai's Kalaupapa after it was discovered he was infected with the disease. His name was Koolau, namesake of the mountains in which Margaret and William walked. Koolau thought the law unjust that would separate him forever from his family and friends. So he gathered his family and a small group of diseased Hawaiians together in Lihue, capital of Kauai, and late one night they fled north into the steep and dangerous mountain valley of Kalalau. The authorities pursued them. In the shadow of NaPali, he killed several of the armed posse and escaped. Koolau was never captured. He died a free man still hiding with his family in the jungle-covered mountains of Kauai.

Margaret looked across the Koolau Mountains and imagined her eighteen-year-old sister Leilani there with a rifle, her hands clawed, her toes falling off, shooting at the police. Margaret thought, too, about the little finger on her own left hand that bent slightly and had no feeling when she pricked it with her darning needle. She wondered if one day, she might join Leilani in the mountains, but she said nothing. The driver waved and honked his horn. The tourists scrambled for the front seats, and Margaret and her father rode down the *pali* in silence.

The inspector from Honolulu's Board of Health in the Kaupuni neighborhood was a tall, skinny man named Kikila. Margaret remembers how he passed up and down the rows of her first-grade class, inspecting children's hands, feet and faces. Then, she thought he was judging them on cleanliness. Proudly she displayed her clean hands and nails. But by the time Margaret was twelve, she had discovered from neighborhood gossip that Kikila was commissioned to look for victims of *ma'i-Pākē*.

One morning, Margaret noticed Kikila walking up and down the dirt strip between her apartment and the asphalt street. Her father had already gone to work and her mother had not returned. Margaret had just walked Robert and Pilahi to school. Apparently, Kikila had seen her there and followed her home. Now, just outside the door, he was waiting to be sure neither of the Kaupuni adults was still present. Health inspectors had a short life expectancy in the streets of Moiliili.

When he knocked at the door, Margaret answered.

"Show me your hands, girl," Kikila ordered.

She remembered that slightly bent finger on her left hand, the one that had no feeling, and held her right hand out to the inspector.

"Now," he demanded, "show me your other hand."

Slowly, she held out her left hand, straining to stretch the little finger even with the others.

"This little finger here," he asked, "it have feeling?"

"Some," she answered.

"Some?" he replied.

"Enough," she assured him.

Kikila paused and looked down at the twelve-year-old.

"Enough, eh?"

Then he turned and was gone. Ida arrived only minutes later. Margaret told her mother that Health Inspector Kikila had paid a visit.

"What for, he come?" she said.

"To look my bent finger, Mama."

"What wrong with finger?" she asked.

"No feeling," Margaret answered.

"No feeling?" For a moment Ida sat stunned by the possibilities. Then she turned and pulled a sewing needle from the little Chinese figure pincushion on the dresser. She grabbed Margaret's hand and, trembling, poked her finger with the needle. A tiny drop of blood formed.

"You feel?"

"No, mama."

Ida poked the child again. This time, the needle went deep.

"You feel that?"

"No, mama."

Ida stared up at Margaret, then rushed to the sink, poured water into a teapot and heated the water until it boiled. She took out a pan from above the sink and put an inch of boiling water at the bottom. She took Margaret's finger and plunged it into the scalding water.

"You feel now?"

"No, mama." Margaret looked at the blisters forming on her finger, but felt nothing.

Ida was stunned silent. Then, suddenly she began to wail. The sob came up from deep inside her as her greatest fears were realized. Margaret, daughter of Edith and Charles, sister of Leilani, had the much feared *ma'i-Pākē*. There was only one hope. Ida dressed in her *Lāpule lole* [Sunday best], left Margaret with the children and caught the number three bus down Kapiolani Boulevard to the Kawaiahao Church. There she would find Sister Sarah Bunker, a deaconess in the church, and arrange with her the *ho'oponopono* for Margaret's illness.

In pre-Christian Hawaiian history, the *ho'oponopono* was a family ceremony conducted by an elder or by a *kahuna*, a holy man, when someone in the family was physically ill or emotionally disturbed. Ida's ancient ancestors believed that at the heart of every sickness was wrongdoing by someone in the family. The *ho'oponopono* was performed to find the problem's root and to make right the wrong in order for healing to begin.

Picture it. Ida's great, great, great, great grandmother [*Kupuna wahine*] lay moaning on her sleeping mat in the bamboo frame hut above Maui's Kahului Bay. From their own huts on the side of Haleakala, her two sons, their wives and children listened to *Kupuna wahine's* misery through the night. When sunrise brought no relief, the family gathered.

"What is wrong with *Kupuna wahine?*" a child whispered.

"Who knows?" answered her mother. "She has been moaning now for three days and nights."

"And my strong *'awa* tea brings no relief," the other woman added. "The taro root and ti leaf wrappings also failed."

"Something more is wrong here than *ma'i kino* [body sickness]," claimed the oldest son. "There is wrongdoing and the *'aumākua* [family gods] are displeased. It is more than *Kupuna wahine's* sickness. Lately, we all have problems. It is time for *ho'oponopono.*"

Without further discussion, the eldest son turned and walked up the mountain trail towards the *kahuna's* hut high on the edge of House of the Sun (Haleakala's crater).

The day was spent in preparation. In small groups and

alone, the family walked above the bay and shared the uneasiness they had felt lately in the family's life together. They wondered aloud what part they might have played in that uneasiness. By nightfall, the oldest son had returned with an old man whose wise, brown eyes smiled out of tawny, wrinkled skin and whose strong, gnarled hands held tightly to a bag filled with special herbs and tiny, carved, wooden forms. The old man spoke in a clear and authoritative voice.

"In the morning, ho'oponopono. Tonight, rest and think about the past."

Then he turned and spread his sleeping mat by the fire and opened the leather bag.

The family watched him set out the tiny wooden statues of his own 'aumākua [gods], then each person wandered away to a sleeping or thinking place to prepare for the morning light.

At sunrise, the family gathered. The kahuna insisted that they eat before ho'oponopono, but the usual sounds of breakfast laughter and conversation were hushed as the family prepared for the ceremony of making right.

When at last they gathered in the nearby hau-covered lānai with its open end facing down across the bay, the mood was serious. The kahuna waited until all the family gathered; then grandmother was carried in and laid on a mat at their feet. In the distance, the sun made a golden, shimmering pathway across the bay. Suddenly, a silhouette appeared on the water. Five fishermen in a long canoe paddled in perfect harmony from the shore out to sea.

The kahuna said, "Look at the fishermen. A family is like them. All is well when we pull together, but when someone stops the rhythm, puts down his paddle or worse, holds it out in the way of the others, the boat will stop and the fish will get away."

Then he spoke directly to the family gods in prayer, "O 'aumakau, listen."

As a younger son to a father, the *kahuna* explained to the gods the problem of the family and asked for help.

When the prayer was over, he turned to grandmother, whose groans of pain had caused the family to gather.

"*Kupuna wahine*, we are here to make right the family wrong that now shows most in you."

Tenderly the old *kahuna* asked the *Kupuna wahine* to say what was troubling her.

Grandmother looked around the circle, her eyes filled with tears, but could not speak.

"I disobeyed grandmother," a young child blurted out. "I left the taro gate open and the *kao* [goat] pulled up many plants."

"You were the one!" said his mother.

"I lied, mama."

Knowing that this child's confession was only the beginning of the process of peeling off *[maīhi]* problems one by one, the *kahuna* asked, "Are you sorry for this wrongdoing?"

"*Ae*," answered the child.

"Will you forgive him, grandma?"

The old woman nodded and the young child threw his arms around her and began to cry.

Throughout the day, there was laughter as petty confessions were made and forgiven. Tempers flared as more serious grievances were discussed and settled. When voices were raised in anger, the *kahuna* interrupted with a prayer. When bodies and minds were tired, the *kahuna* asked that food be served and rest taken. Layer after layer of wrongdoing was uncovered. Still grandma couldn't speak. Finally, in a hush, they heard her whisper, "*pololū* [long spear]."

A grandson in his late teens gasped and turned pale. The circle grew silent. Each face turned in his direction. Hesitantly, he began his confession.

"I stole the *pololū*, father, and sold it to the *hui Kalepa* [the trading store]."

The long spear was a family treasure passed on to his father by the boy's ancestors over more than a hundred years. Trading companies knew collectors would pay high prices for *pololū*. They gave the boy almost nothing for it. His father, who valued the spear as a treasured part of his heritage, was enraged. The grandmother began to cry. She had seen her grandson take the *pololū* and carry it down the mountain to Kipahulu. The *kahuna* looked at the sobbing youth.

"Are you sorry that you stole the *pololū?*"

"*Ae*, I am very sorry, father."

"Will you forgive your son?"

Slowly the angry parent whispered, "*Ae.*"

Then, detail by detail, the agreement was reached whereby the guilty boy would pay for his wrongdoing. The *ho'oponopono* had created an opportunity for the family to pool their spiritual and emotional resources. During those long two days of soul-searching, the current problems within the family were exposed and treated through forgiveness. At the close of *ho'oponopono*, the *kahuna* prescribed herbal treatments to restore grandma's weakened body. Then he packed up his leather bag and returned to his home high on Haleakala's cloud-enshrouded crater.

In the ancient, pre-Christian times of Ida's ancestry, this ceremony for making right was taken with ultimate seriousness. There was more at stake than one person's health. The entire family's welfare was jeopardized by the disharmony that was causing the illness. Suffering was a sign that pointed to a far more serious wrong. The root of the wrong must be uncovered by the family and the wrong must be made right through the process of confession and forgiveness. No one dared lie during *ho'oponopono* before the elders, the *kahuna* and the family gods assembled. For unless the hurt could be healed, the suffering would spread from one family to the whole tribe. In order to make right, heal the family and even save the nation, the guilty person confessed his wrong in *ho'oponopono*. The family made the arrangements by which the guilty person could make right the wrongdoing and, after punishment by the family, if the crime was serious he would be turned over to the village elders for penalties as painful as banishment or death.

The early Christian Hawaiians recognized the truth behind *ho'oponopono* and continued the practice, but with a significant new Christian dimension. They believed that in the life, death and resurrection of Jesus, all wrong had been forgiven forever. God had paid the price for people's wrongdoing in the sacrificial death of Jesus. Therefore, the Christian could promise new hope to the person who confessed in *ho'oponopono*. God would forgive and through His grace, the wrong could be made right and the wrongdoer restored to life again.

With this hope, Ida got off that bus down Kapiolani Avenue, hurried to the row of offices behind the great coral Kawaiahao Church and knocked on the door of Sarah Bunker's little office. The tall, dark-skinned Hawaiian deaconess opened the door and smiled.

"Ida, *komo mai* [come inside]."

For a moment Ida stood numbly in the doorway. She could not blink away the tears that washed her eyes and gradually trickled down her cheeks.

"Tell me, Ida. How can we help you?" Sarah Bunker put her arm around Ida's shoulder and led her gently to a wicker chair. Ida wiped her nose with the handkerchief Sarah offered and slowly spoke.

"Margaret very sick. Need *ho'oponopono!*"

That same night while Ida and Sarah Bunker made arrangements for *ho'oponopono*, Margaret stood with a giggling chorus of twelve-year-old girls in Auntie Keaka's advanced hula class, draping their special guest in handmade ginger and plumeria leis. The warm brown eyes of the tall, graceful woman with her crown of silvery gray hair smiled down as young arms encircled her and young lips brushed her cheeks with affection. Iolani was a giant calm in the center of this storm of adulation. She was *ali'i kumu hula*, Hawaii's reigning hula queen. Ancient Polynesian dances were stored in the old woman's brain and recreated as if by magic in the movements of the boys and girls she taught. Her students had danced before royalty around the world. For her to visit a neighborhood hula class in Auntie Keaka's humble house was a great surprise, but the news she brought Margaret and her friends outsurprised her presence.

The girls from Moiliili had been chosen to dance before the 1934 May Queen in the Hale Honolulu, the great open-air reception hall of Honolulu's City Hall. Iolani would coach them in the final preparation for their performance of the hula *Kā'eke'eke*, a dance selected by her for the occasion.

Suddenly, Auntie Keaka raised her hand. A row of young men wearing tapa loin clothes and carrying long bamboo poles entered the room. They dropped to their knees in two rows facing each other, holding opposite ends of the *kā'eke'eke* poles. Auntie Keaka escorted Iolani to the cracked and faded chair of honor, then stood proudly beside her teacher as the girls took their places among the poles.

The boys hit the wooden floor simultaneously with the *kā'eke'ekes* to signal the dance had begun. The poles were in varying sizes from two feet to six feet in length. Each pole had one end cut open. The boys played the poles by tapping them rhythmically on the floor or ground. The girls danced gingerly among the poles in perfect time to the ancient rhythms and haunting sounds of the *kā'eke'eke*. The dance began without a flaw. Right legs in. Tap, tap, tap. Left legs in. Tap, tap, tap. Faster and faster the poles were tapped and faster and faster the young girls danced.

Then everything went wrong. Stepping backwards, one girl's heel hit an ascending pole. She strained to regain her balance as her other foot fell directly beneath a descending pole with a bruising blow. She staggered. Another girl reached out to steady her but in turn, tripped out of rhythm. The two girls crashed into each other and fell. Others jumped back and stumbled over poles or the boys holding them. The dance ended in a tangle of bodies and bamboo at Iolani's feet.

Nobody moved. Auntie Keaka was too stunned and embarrassed to speak. The girls leaned in terror on hands and elbows or knelt in awkward silence. All eyes were on Iolani. She looked down at them, her eyes barely seeing over the mountain of leis they had draped around her neck. The only sound in the room was the sound her fingers made still tapping out the rhythms of the *Kāʻekeʻeke* on the rickety arm of auntie's antique chair.

Then Iolani laughed, quietly, to herself.

"I remember," she said softly, "I remember the bruise on my right big toe when I first danced under a *kāʻekeʻeke*. I was a young girl then, like you, and I was afraid my toe nail would stay blue forever."

The stately woman leaned down from her chair, recalling memories half a century old to calm and console these girls only a dozen years alive.

"I remember, too, the first time I made the *kai pupule* [the motion of the raging sea] and poked my teacher in the eye."

With this picture of the greatest teacher of them all poking her own teacher in the eye, even auntie had to smile. Then, slowly, Iolani stood to her feet and walked directly to the little girl whose painful mistake had caused the catastrophe. She was easy to spot, for tears ran down her cheeks and her body shook with silent sobs. The old woman put her arms around the girl and lifted her up. With a large, silk handkerchief she wiped the tears away. Then, taking the girl by the hand, Iolani led her back towards the musicians still holding the *kā'eke'eke* in readiness. The great Iolani looked down one last time at the twelve-year-old from Moiliili and then she signaled the boys to begin the dance again.

"Tap!" the poles signal in unison.

"Tap! Tap! Tap!" the ancient rhythm began, and side by side the little girl and old woman began to dance. Right leg in. Tap. Tap. Tap. Left leg in. Tap. Tap. Tap. Faster and faster the poles played their song and faster and faster the child and Iolani danced. She held her long muumuu in her hands only inches above the floor. Not once did she look at the poles crashing at her feet. Not once did she even glance with any sign of nervousness at the little girl who caused her first partner's fall.

Iolani looked straight ahead. Her eyes were closed. For that moment she was the embodiment of centuries of her people singing their song across the green mountains and blue seas of the ancient islands. Faster she danced until she was as one with those young brown arms and their flashing bamboo poles. The girls watched with open-mouthed amazement. Auntie Keaka beamed, for the great Iolani was dancing again, and her girls were there to see it. Then, with a final crash of the *kā'eke'ekes*, the dance ended. Iolani bowed low to her now-smiling partner whose tears had long since been forgotten. The little girl bowed back.

"Remember," whispered Iolani to the child so they all would hear, "when you fall, take only a short time to cry. Then jump right up and dance again."

In the years ahead, Margaret would remember.

Promptly at 6:00 P.M. the following night, Ida led her family up the stairs of Kawaiahao Church.

"Not enough we come church Sunday," protested William. "Now only Wednesday we back again."

"*Kuli kuli!* [Be quiet]," answered Ida. "Sarah Bunker hear! Very nice to do *ho'oponopono* for Margaret tonight."

Margaret guided Robert and Pilahi into the semi-darkened church behind her father.

"Sit here. Wait. I go bring Sarah Bunker."

William was still growling his protest when the two women returned. He had already downed a six-pack of Primo in two separate bars between the Honolulu Iron Works and their apartment in Moiliili to ease his fears about Margaret and this *ho'oponopono* business. William didn't believe in God and he didn't care much for ancient Hawaiian traditions either, especially mid-week after ten hours on the charging machine at the iron works.

Sarah Bunker entered the empty row in front of the family, sat down and leaned informally over the pew back towards them. It was then she told them the story of the stolen *pololū* and the *ho'oponopono* held to make it right. As the story ended she said,

"Now we will all pray for Margaret."

The family bowed reverently. Margaret still remembers how she trembled that night when, alone with her family and Sarah Bunker in that great church where Hawaiian royalty worshiped, she heard her own name echoed in prayer.

"Father, we are here to assist in the healing of Margaret Kaupuni and her family. Be here with us. Help us make right with you and with each other. In Jesus' name. Amen."

William put his head back against the pew at the beginning of the prayer and was asleep before it ended. Gently, Sarah Bunker awakened William.

"God not heal my baby!" he said, barely awake. "Why we waste time here?"

Margaret remembers that Sarah Bunker tried to explain to William that whether God chose to heal his daughter or not, this process of making right would help to heal all of them and give them new strength to face the future together. In Margaret's words, "Sarah Bunker say, 'William, Margaret have one terrible *ma'i*. Nobody know why she have. Nobody know how she going get betta. We make right with God and family. Be strong that way. Leave the rest to God.'

"Then Ida began to cry. 'Baby,' she said to me, 'forgive mama for the wrong she done you? She lick you every time and this and that. You know. Please forgive!'

"I say, 'All right, mama. I forgive.' And mama come over by me, put her head on my shoulder and cry and say, 'O, tank you, baby. I so sorry.'

"Then William, he say, '*Kuli kuli*. God not heal baby.' And he laugh loud and hit one pew with his hands. Then he stop laughing and get real mad. He swear at Sarah Bunker and at my mama. Robert and Pilahi start to cry. Sarah Bunker say soft, 'This house of God. No talk any kind funny now. We need make right.'

"William yell at mama again. Mama cry. Sarah Bunker put arm around Ida and begin to pray. Everybody get quiet again. William go back to sleep. End Sarah Bunker's prayer, she slide down pew until right in front of William. He was snoring loud.

"'William?' she say, real loud for church. My father woke up and saw this big Hawaiian lady leaning over him.

"'William!' she tell him again. 'Maybe you the root of this problem.'

"William look at that lady for long time but nevah go back to sleep.

"'Maybe God need heal you more than Margaret. You fight all the time with Ida. You hit Ida and children. Maybe Margaret sick to get away from you!'

"William wide awake now," continued Margaret. "First time he think maybe he be part of problem. He looked at me. I shaking bad. Then he look at Ida. She real mad. Then William talk soft, like whisper,

"'I'm sorry, mama,' he told her. 'You forgive me?'

"Ida look the other way. No forgive. Then Sarah Bunker say to mama in Hawaiian, '*A ole make kekanaka nokaheva aka no kamihi ole.*' That means: Man does not die because of his sin but because he does not forgive.

"Long time Ida wait. William say again, 'I sorry. Please forgive me, baby. What you like me do to make right?'

"Ida look him in the eye and say, 'You marry me. Things be right for Margaret then!'

"William say, 'O.K., baby, we get married.'

"'Then I forgive you,' Mama said and she climb right over me and the kids and hug William good.

"Then William look over mama at me and say, 'Will you forgive me, too, baby, for all the times I beat you and all that?'

"I say to William just like I say to mama, 'All right, daddy, I forgive.'"

Ida and William were married several months later in their little apartment in Moiliili. Margaret didn't see the wedding: it came a few weeks too late. On May Day, 1934, she was taken away from her family and friends to the Kalihi Receiving Station. She would not return to Moiliili for thirty-three years.

That day began as the happiest day in Margaret's young life. She would join Auntie Keaka's class on the portable stage erected in the great court of the Honolulu Hale. She and her other twelve-year-old friends would dance before the May Queen, her court and the officials of the city. Her father had to work that day. But Margaret remembers that she wore a skirt of thirty ti leaves that William had collected and sewn together and mock orange leaves he had pounded until they looked like a royal *maile* lei. Her mother didn't feel well and stayed in bed while her daughter danced. But Margaret remembers wearing a fluffy red top that Ida had cut and stitched from expensive material especially for this occasion.

The young men in tapa cloth and plumeria leis ran smartly into place. Simultaneoulsy, the *kāʻekeʻekes* in their hands tapped out the ancient rhythms. And Margaret and her friends began to dance. Right foot in. Tap. Tap. Tap. Left foot in. Tap Tap. Tap. Faster and faster the sound echoed. Faster and faster the girls danced. Then, all too suddenly, it was over. Iolani stood and led the applause. All the little girls were crying as the audience clapped and waved and smiled up at them. As Margaret rushed from the stage, her face flushed by that one, brief moment of praise, a tall, thin man reached out a bony hand, grasped Margaret's arm and steered her away from the other dancers. She recognized Mr. Kikila, the Health Inspector. She guessed why he was there. But she had no idea of the long-range horror in the news he brought that day.

"You are a leper, child, and you will come with me."

The Kawaihao Church, Hawaii's Westminster Cathedral. Margaret attended this church as a child. Here, deaconess Sarah Bunker led Margaret's family in the *ho'oponopono* service seeking God's guidance and healing for Margaret's leprosy. (Photo by Joe F. Konno.)

Margaret at age five.

Margaret at age nine.

Margaret's neighborhood hula class was chosen to dance before the May Queen in 1934. At the close of her performance, she was confronted by a health inspector and taken to the Kalihi Receiving Station where her leprosy was confirmed. (Photo courtesy of the State Archives of Hawaii.)

Left: Margaret at age twelve just before she was taken to the Kalihi Receiving Station and diagnosed as having leprosy. Note the slight deformities already apparent in her hands. It was Margaret's fingers that caused the Department of Health inspector to be suspicious of her health.

Right: Bessie "Ma" Clinton. This is the only known picture of "Ma" Clinton, the compassionate administrator of Kalihi Hospital—the half-way house for leprosy patients en route to Molokai. (Photo courtesy of the State Archives of Hawaii.)

AERIAL VIEW OF KALIHI HOSPITAL. HONOLULU

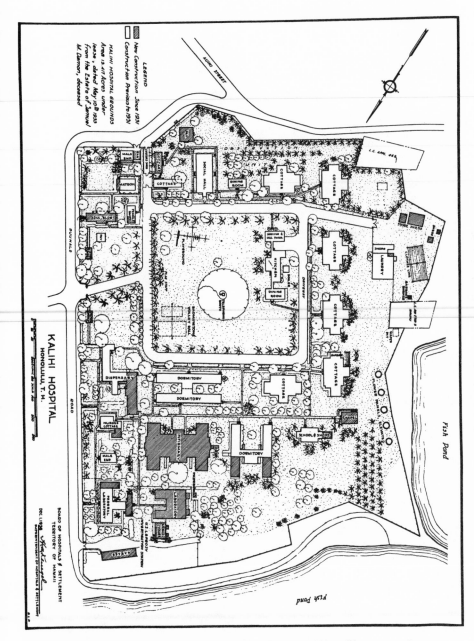

(Photos on these two pages are coutesy of the State Archives of Hawaii.)

Above: "Ma" Clinton's Chapel, Kalihi Receiving Station, Honolulu, Hawaii. When the Public Health Department didn't have resources to build the patients a chapel on the grounds of the hospital, "Ma" Clinton, the hospital staff and patients built their own chapel. **Below:** Happy Home School, Kalihi Receiving Station, Honolulu, Hawaii. Behind the high walls and guarded gates of the Receiving Station, Margaret attended Happy Home School with the other leprosy-afflicted children before being shipped to Molokai. (Photos courtesy of the State Archives of Hawaii.)

II.

KALIHI RECEIVING STATION HOSPITAL

1934–36

Health Inspector Kikila drove in silence down Punchbowl Street past the Kawaiahao Church, across Queen to Ala Moana Boulevard.

"You want candy?" he asked the twelve-year-old girl still wearing her hula skirt and the mock orange lei.

"All right," she answered. He reached into the glove box and pulled out a bag of sticky Japanese rice candy and handed Margaret the bag. As she removed the cellophane wrapper, she asked him, "Where we go?"

"First," answered Kikila, "we're going to pick up Leilani at your mother's."

"Leilani?" Margaret asked surprised. "How you catch her too?"

"Then," Kikila answered, ignoring her question, "we're going for one long ride."

That one long ride up King Street to Dillingham Boulevard past Honolulu Harbor and Sand Island ended just south of the Oahu Prison on Sand Island Road. The Kalihi Receiving Station stood on a triangular spit of land jutting out into the Keehi Lagoon. It was the next to last stop for those on their way to Kalaupapa, the leprosarium on Molokai. Kikila had driven dozens of men, women and children to Kalihi. Few of them would return. To families unaffected by leprosy, the Health Inspector was a coura-

geous knight riding his old yellow Chevy about the town
ridding the land of the "plague" and those who bore it in
their bodies. To the families of victims of the illness, Kikila
was a bounty hunter, who was paid ten dollars a 'head' to
snatch innocent people and carry them away to living
death.

Leprosy was then and is now mildly contagious, but the
danger of catching it from another person has been greatly
exaggerated. Very few persons exposed to the disease
develop it. Leprosy develops in less than five percent of
those persons married to leprosy patients. There are
almost no cases among the doctors and nurses who care for
leprosy patients. Now leprosy can be rendered inactive,
arrested and cured, but when Kikila picked up Margaret
and Leilani, little was known and much was feared about
the disease. Late in the nineteenth century, the Legislature of the Territory of Hawaii had decreed that diagnosed
victims must be isolated immediately from the general
public. Kikila was simply a much-maligned instrument of
that legislation.

The inspector's car stopped in front of Margaret's
mother's home on Kukui Street in Iwilei. Kikila brushed
past the protesting woman at the door, entered the little
wood frame, tar-paper-roofed home and emerged with a
nineteen-year-old girl holding a newborn baby in her arms.

"Mama, you take baby," Leilani said, choking back her
tears. She handed the weeks old infant to the confused
woman and walked beside Kikila to the car.

"I'll be back, mama. Bye, bye, Keiki. See you tonight."

Leilani opened the car door and was surprised to find her
sister sitting in the front seat.

"Margaret, why you here?"

"I leper too, Leilani. We go Kalihi together. Come. He
give you candy."

Kikila climbed in the front seat and started the car.
Leilani shouted at him from the back seat.

"You steal babies with candy. You nothing but 'aihue

[thief]. I no got *maʻi-Pākē*. You'll see. I going back home wit Keiki tonight."

Leilani began to cry. Margaret sucked the sticky candy and looked up over the dashboard at the passing sights. Kikila drove the long road to Kalihi. His car was signaled in past the sentry at the gate. The yellow Chevy braked before a long sloping ramp that led to the Kalihi Hospital. Kikila signed a paper for the admitting nurse. And after his passengers were taken from the car, he turned and drove back toward Honolulu.

Another nurse greeted the two girls kindly and led them to a hospital room. There, she instructed Margaret to take off the clothes she had worn in the May Day celebration— the precious hula skirt William had made from thirty ti leaves, the *maile*-like lei of mock orange leaves and the bright red top Ida had made from new, store-bought cloth. The nurse scooped up Margaret's treasures, put them in a paper bag and before the little girl could protest, dumped them into a nearby trash container.

Margaret turned to her sister and asked, "Why she do that?"

Leilani sat dazed on the edge of the bed.

"I no *maʻi-Pākē*," she said, over and over to herself. "Tonight I going back to my Kieki. You see."

Margaret, beginning to feel cold, asked, "Leilani, what we wear here?" Leilani didn't answer.

The nurse returned and helped both girls into their hospital smocks with only the strings that tie in back to keep out the breeze. She handed them each two cups of liquid.

"You drink both cups. Don't worry. This one is Epsom salts, and this one will help clean you out for the tests tomorrow."

"What you mean, 'tomorrow'? I have baby, I must go home, take care."

"Oh, you can't go home today, child," answered the Hawaiian nurse gently. "You will have tests this week, and if the tests are negative, you may go home," she hesitated, "before long. Now drink your medicine like good girls."

The nurse turned and walked quickly from the room.

Leilani shouted after her, "What you mean, 'before long'? How long?" But the door swung silently closed.

Leilani never went home, nor did she ever see her child again. The tests the doctors would perform over those next long months were only to confirm what they already knew from earlier tests taken when Leilani was at a hospital in childbirth. Margaret's leprosy had not yet been confirmed.

That afternoon, a young *haole* doctor made a small cut in Margaret's finger and on her ear with a scalpel, scraped a small sample of fluid and smeared it on a clean glass slide. Nurses dried the slide by passing it over a flame. Then they stained the sample with red and blue dyes.

A Norwegian scientist, Gerhard Hansen, first isolated and identified the leprosy germ under a microscope in 1873. Now the disease and the bacterium that carry it are sometimes called by his name. Hansen's bacillus resists acid. Under the microscope the acid-treated bacilli become noticeably pinkish. The seriousness of the disease is directly related to the number of pink bacteria present. Both Margaret's and Leilani's smears proved positive.

Within hours of their children's legal abduction, the families began to gather at the Kalihi Gate. Ida arrived first, swearing vengeance on Inspector Kikila. "I going break his body and feed um to da dogs!" she swore. When William came directly from the Iron Works, he tried to calm his wife; but she was already invoking ancient Hawaiian curses on the inspector. Then Edith and Charles arrived together. It was impossible for their girls to receive visitors that first day, so all four parents gathered at Asaki's Store and Cafe nearby.

"How Kikila know Margaret sick?" Ida wondered aloud

over a cold drink at Asaki's. "She not in school. She no take test. How he find out?"

Edith looked down at her drink. She said nothing. Ida noticed Edith's strange reaction and asked again, this time directly, "You know how Kikila find out Margaret sick?"

Edith looked up, began to speak, then stopped and turned away again.

"You told!" Ida screamed at her. "You told Kikila Margaret sick!"

"Leilani my first baby," Edith said quietly. "Not right she go Kalaupapa alone."

Ida howled across the table, "How can you do that?" Then she put her head down and began to cry. Soon Edith and the two men were also crying. They spent that evening crying and drinking and shouting invectives at Kikila and at each other. Then they piled into a battered taxi and went home to bed.

The families didn't know it, but Margaret did have one visitor that first day. Sarah Bunker, the deaconess from Kawaiahao Church, heard that Margaret was at Kalihi. The moment she heard the news, she wrapped a book in tapa cloth, borrowed the custodian's car, and drove the long ride to the Kalihi Receiving Station. The guards waved her through on sight. They knew Sarah Bunker; she had been there many times before.

Sarah walked quickly through the long corridors of the Kalihi Hospital until she found Margaret's room. The little girl was sitting alone, looking out the window, when Sarah Bunker arrived. The old woman sat on the bed beside her, put her arm around her and said, "Margaret, I brought you a present."

Eagerly Margaret unwrapped the tapa cloth and found a leather-covered Hawaiian Bible just like Ida's.

"Wherever you go, child, carry this book. Read it. *Ho'opa'ana'au* [memorize]. Keep it in your heart."

Then the tall, gray-haired Hawaiian Christian lady knelt

beside Margaret's bed and began to pray. Margaret still remembers the strength that Sarah Bunker's visit gave her over the years ahead. Forty years later, she still has that Hawaiian Bible. It is dog-eared and frayed from much reading. It was then and is now a sign that Sarah Bunker cared, that Sarah Bunker's God had not forgotten her.

To tell the truth, Margaret liked Kalihi. It was a relief to be away from Ida and William, their violent quarrels and painful beatings. It was a pleasure to have free time from baby-sitting Robert and Pilahi, from washing dishes and scrubbing floors, from cleaning fish and straining poi. That first new day at the hospital Margaret felt like she was in a resort hotel on some fancy vacation.

The orderly brought her new clothes after breakfast on her first morning at the Kalihi Receiving Station. Margaret slipped into the rather large but new skirt and matching blouse the government provided her. A nurse entered the room and found her dressed and waiting.

"Good morning, Margaret. Are you ready for breakfast?"

Margaret looked dazed. Breakfast at home was something she prepared and ate alone. William would have left for the early morning shift and Ida was usually sound asleep, still in her cannery uniform, too tired to undress.

"Yes. Ready," Margaret answered.

"You look very nice," the nurse added. "'Ma' Clinton is anxious to meet you."

Together they walked down the halls of the hospital and out across the closely cropped grass of the Kalihi Receiving Station. The hospital stood at the center of the complex. From its upper stories you could see the ocean and the palm trees along white sand beaches in the distance.

"That is Hale Hoikiana, the girls' building," the nurse

pointed at a long, green dormitory where the single girls lived.

"Across the way," she added, "is the boys' building. And there is Mother's Building where our married couples live. You aren't married, are you?"

The nurse grinned down at twelve-year-old Margaret and Margaret felt her face flush.

"No, I nevah marry," she replied.

"We'll see," said the nurse, smiling.

Just then a pleasant young Hawaiian man walked across the campus toward them.

"Mr. Albert, I would like you to meet one of our new patients," called the nurse. "Margaret, this is Mr. Albert, the teacher in Mount Happy Home School."

"Good morning, Margaret."

Mr. Albert held out a very crippled hand. Margaret looked up at his face and then down at his clawlike hand, her hands at her side. For a moment, she remembered her daydream of Leilani in the mountain with claw hands and a rifle. Finally, Mr. Albert dropped his hand and smiled.

"It was nice to meet you, Margaret. We'll get better acquainted in class. See you then."

Margaret and the nurse walked on towards the cafeteria.

"What's wrong with his hand?" Margaret asked. "It look funny, like *'awe'awe* [octopus tentacle]."

"Mr. Albert is also a patient here, Margaret. His hands were damaged by his disease. Forget them. He is a very nice man and an excellent teacher. That's what is important."

"My hands going look like that some day?" Margaret asked.

The nurse looked down at Margaret, started to reply, then walked on without a word. They entered the administration building and walked up a brightly lit corridor to the office of Mrs. Bessie Clinton. "Ma" Clinton ran Kalihi like an admiral runs a battleship in wartime. She was a large-boned, gray-haired *haole* who prided herself on strict discipline, but she cared about each patient and worked tirelessly to help in their recovery.

"Good morning, Margaret. Sit down, won't you?"

Mrs. Clinton looked through Margaret's folder for a moment and then glanced up at her over wire-rimmed glasses.

"Says here you are one fine hula dancer."

Margaret smiled. "Yes. I study *Kā'eke'eke* with Iolani."

"Did you *unike* [graduate her hula course]?" asked "Ma" Clinton.

"No, I no *unike* yet. I come ovah here instead."

"Ma" Clinton looked back at the file, then up at Margaret. "It also says here that you quit school when you were only six. Why was that?"

"I no like," Margaret answered.

"Ma" Clinton closed the file, stood and walked around the desk.

"Margaret, you have a serious disease, but people who have leprosy don't die from it. They die because they refuse to take their medicine or continue their treatments. They 'no like,' as you said. So they get lazy, careless. They catch other diseases more serious. Their body can't fight two wars at the same time. So they die."

She got down on one knee before the child and looked her in the eye.

"Child, we can help you if you obey the rules, take your medicine, finish your tests and treatments every day." She paused. "Even if you 'no like.' Understand?"

"*Ae*," whispered Margaret.

"Good," added "Ma" Clinton; then she smiled the smile that hundreds of patients at Kalihi still remember. "Don't worry. We are all here to help you get better. And if you help us do it, we'll succeed. Now, how about some breakfast?"

Again, "Ma" Clinton smiled at Margaret. The little girl did not return the smile but stood expressionless, her hands at her side, feeling the strength of this great woman and, strangely, at the same time feeling her love. Then, the two of them walked across the campus to the cafeteria. "Ma" Clinton left her in the breakfast line with all the other patients. As she waved good-bye, she said to Margaret, "Remember, if you need anything, my door is always open. *Aloha.*"

Margaret watched "Ma" Clinton stride quickly back to her office. Then, the little girl turned to join the other patients in the line. The first thing Margaret noticed was how many of them had claw-like hands similar to Mr. Albert's. Their skin looked puffy, with large, protruding bumps on their faces and arms and funny ear lobes that looked like they'd been stretched. These patients were all in the early stages of leprosy. Some, like Margaret, had almost no signs of the disease. The girl who stood in line in front of her had no blemishes at all.

"Hello," the girl said, "you new? I Carrie."

"Hi," Margaret answered. "You leper, too?"

"My tests positive. I got plenty bugs on me, dey say, but no sign they do anything yet. You?"

"I got one little finger with no feeling," Margaret answered. "How old you?"

"I eleven," Carrie replied. "But already in fourt grade at Mount Happy Home School. 'Mount Sick Home' we call 'um."

The girls laughed. About that time, Margaret and Carrie reached the front of the line. Margaret was scooping up rice and gravy and fried potatoes when a short, round *haole* with her hair in a little mesh net bustled up and leaned over the counter.

"Good morning. You must be new. Remember, all that starch will make you fat as a dirigible. Here, let me get your breakfast."

Carrie almost doubled over, choking back her laughter.

"Dat Miss Oldin. She dietician. Look out. She make you eat good and dat ain't good."

Miss Oldin bustled back with a plate loaded high with eggs and bacon, a large bowl of a runny red and lumpy substance and a glass of milk.

"Here you are, young woman. Remember, you are what you eat. Let's get you well and out of here. Rice and gravy just won't do it."

With that, she bustled off on another unrequested errand of mercy, looking after her charges like a busy mother hen. Margaret looked down at the dish of red slime on her plate and asked Carrie, "What that?"

Carrie looked very serious for a moment and answered "Dis da leftovers from da operating room."

Margaret turned pale and then both girls giggled. However, it wasn't long until Margaret discovered that Miss Oldin's kitchen was a very important part of getting well. Besides, even the stewed tomatoes tasted good after what she would drink that day and every day during the years that followed.

Chaulmoogra oil treatments were prescribed for Margaret at her first hospital appointment immediately after breakfast. She broke open the chaulmoogra capsule, poured the oil into a teaspoon, gagged down the medicine and wished she were eating Miss Oldin's stewed tomatoes. The thick, oily substance was refined from the bark of the hydnocarpus tree. It was taken by mouth and injected into the victim as well.

It was Mr. Albert who later explained in class that, for centuries, there was no medicine for victims of the disease. Leprosy victims were cast out of their homes and villages. The first recorded disease in antiquity, leprosy promised its victims horrible deformities and a long, sure death. The afflicted wrapped their oozing, ugly sores in rags. Their fingers and toes, hands, feet and faces seemed to rot away. They were the untouchables, required by law to cry, "Unclean! Unclean!" to those they passed. Leprosy victims bore the marks of the walking dead. Cut off from human contact, shamed and crippled by their disease, victims became the subjects of fear and prejudice.

Then, after the millennia of hopelessness, chaulmoogra oil was discovered.

Now sulfone drugs arrest and cure the disease. But sulfone drugs were discovered ten years after Margaret entered Kalihi. Her hope lay in that awful, sticky stuff with the unpronounceable name in the capsule held in her trembling hand.

The little girl in her oversized dress sat in the waiting room; her feet dangled above the floor. She was surrounded by older patients also waiting for their tests or treatments. She watched their bent and crippled hands in fascination, then looked down at her own young hands, perfect except for one numb, slightly bent finger.

"Margaret Kaupuni?"

A nurse entered the room and called her name. Margaret stood and walked into a little office and sat down on the cold, metal chair. For one fleeting moment, she saw in another office across the hall a man whose face looked like a checkerboard. Then the doctor entered and closed the door.

"Why that man over there have one black-and-white face?" Margaret asked.

The doctor tried to explain the treatment that she too would undergo during the next two-and-one-half years at Kalihi.

"Margaret, inside your skin, tiny little germs are attacking the healthy nerves and inflaming them. Your finger is an example. We have to stop those little fires and keep the germs from spreading. Have you ever seen the forest in the hills above Honolulu?"

Margaret had.

"Well," continued the doctor, "when the forests burn, firefighters attack the flames and clear an area around the fire to keep the fire from spreading. We inject chaulmoogra oil into your skin around the little germs to stop the inflammation and to keep the bacilli from spreading and attacking any more of your healthy nerve tissue.

"That man across the hall has been having injections of chaulmoogra oil for several months. Every day, we inject dozens of little squirts of oil around the diseased areas on his face. Little by little, the oil spots join under his skin, drowning the germs and helping the injured nerves repair themselves again."

It was difficult for Margaret to understand the treatment. But everyday, understand or not, she grimaced and drank the oil from that little capsule. Weekly she reported to the doctor where she received her injections of that same oil.

Months went by. The painful treatments continued. And little by little Margaret got worse. Still it was difficult to see any signs of the disease on her almost perfect body. Other patients had more obvious symptoms. Some were injected hundreds and hundreds of times every week. Day after day, month after month, they returned for the injections. The doctors attacked different patches on their skin with the needles, willing to cover all of the body if necessary. It might take tens of thousands of injections to do the job. Sometimes there were great signs of improvement. Ugly, patchy faces were restored to semi-normalcy. Great nodules on the arms and legs disappeared and normal-looking skin returned. Others reacted violently to the treatment and were made worse by it.

But life at Kalihi was not only stewed tomatoes and chaulmoogra oil. Margaret and her friend Carrie, the youngest patients at the Receiving Station, had devised a hundred ways to divert themselves. After years of hard work and adult responsibility, it was a time of freedom for Margaret, and she made the most of it. Every month each girl received $20 allowance from the government to buy clothing and to cover the costs of incidentals such as extra school materials, entertainment and junk food purchased outside the cafeteria, away from Miss Oldin's intimidating gaze.

Asaki's Store and Cafe stood just outside the high wire wall that encircled the Kalihi Receiving Station. He had devised an ingenious electronic bell that patients could ring for service. Mr. Asaki, his wife or one of his children, upon hearing the bell, would run across the street, bow two or three times in greeting, and ask the patient standing behind the wire wall for his or her order. Margaret was especially fond of Asaki's huli-huli chicken, juicy pieces of leg or breast grilled in its own juices on a constantly turning spit in Asaki's kitchen. After writing down the patient's order, Asaki's waiters would run back across the busy street, wrap the huli-huli in foil and return to serve the patient. At the hole in the fence, Asaki had permanently mounted a large, glass mayonnaise jar filled with alcohol. To pay for the chicken, the patient dropped his money into the alcohol. Asaki's waiters retrieved it, thanked the customer with several more quick bows, then returned to work. Or, if the patient preferred, Asaki would serve on credit. Margaret often hoarded her allowance and on her Saturday visits, Ida would pay the bill.

Margaret and Carrie returned to their little room at Hale Hoikiana to eat their chicken and dream their secret dreams of escape from Kalihi Hospital. One night, they turned their dreams to action.

"Give me that *'aki* [pillow]," Margaret ordered in a loud whisper. "I stuff it here under the covers. David and Kikino no can tell. They nevah come in here anyway."

David and Kikino were watchmen who patrolled the

grounds at night. When Margaret first saw the men patrolling the grounds, she asked Carrie if they were there to keep bad people out. Carrie laughed and said, "What bad people come here? Must be crazy. No. David and Kikino here to keep us in."

It was the first time Margaret understood fully that she was a prisoner in Kalihi. Her bed was soft and warm. Miss Oldin's food was filling. The clothes were fine. But when Margaret realized that she was trapped like a criminal, she began to plan her first escape.

"But Margaret, people stay scared of us out dere. Dey think we give 'em *ma'i-Pākē*. Police come. Take us back anyway."

But the dream grew. That night Margaret convinced her friend that escape was possible. They planned to return before sunrise so that no one would ever know the difference.

"Put clothes on the chair and toss 'em on the end of the bed."

"But how we going get over da wall?" Carrie asked, excited, but unsure of Margaret's plan.

"We climb hau tree across from Asaki's."

"Then how we going get back?"

"We climb back. You scared?"

"No. We go. My mother happy fo'a see us. She no care we out. What we going do dere?"

Then Margaret told her the full plan.

"We catch one bus to Waikiki, walk up and down Kalakaua Avenue, see Claudette Colbert movie and come back here before anybody know!"

It was a most un-Margaret-like plan, but she had been working on it for months and Carrie whistled under her breath in admiration.

The great escape worked without a hitch. Margaret and Carrie waited until David and Kikino made their rounds and returned to the guardhouse for coffee. Then, shoes in hand, they made a run for the large hau tree, climbed it in the darkness, dropped down onto the sidewalk and ran for Sand Island Road. A bus picked them up almost immediately and they were off on their adventure. After dinner at Carrie's mom's house and a movie on Ala Moana Boulevard, they walked up and down Kalakaua Avenue with its grand tourist hotels fronting on Waikiki beach and its expensive nightclubs and restaurants. As the girls passed the Royal Hawaiian Hotel, they heard the throbbing beat of the *kā'eke-'eke*. Margaret froze.

"What's a matta, Margaret? You seen ghost?"

Margaret listened, then turned and walked past the elegant Hawaiian doorman into the main lobby of the impressive pink landmark in the center of Waikiki.

"Where you going, Margaret? They catch you in dere, make luau pig of your head."

For a few frantic moments, Carrie stood alone on the busy sidewalk, then ran to join her determined friend. Margaret strode through the lobby like a guest with a penthouse key. Carrie walked tall beside her whispering to Margaret out of the corner of her mouth, "You going get us killed. What we going do if they catch us?"

"I tell them we lepers," Margaret answered, "and if they touch we give them *ma'i-Pākē.*"

Then Margaret stopped beneath the lobby's great wooden arches and looked down across the tourists sipping chichis and eating *pūpū* [Hawaiian hors d'oeuvres]. Young men wearing only tapa loin clothes and flowers were beating the stage with *kā'eke'eke* poles. Beautiful young girls, like Margaret, danced across the poles. Right foot in. Tap. Tap. Tap. Left foot in. Tap. Tap. Tap. Faster and faster they danced. Then, in the lobby of the Royal Hawaiian Hotel, unnoticed by staff or tourists, a little girl dressed in oversized clothes began to dance the rhythms of the *kā'eke'eke*, the awful thought growing in her head that she might never dance again.

It was David who noticed Margaret and Carrie jumping up and down outside the Kalihi fence trying to snare an overhanging branch of the hau tree. It wasn't difficult to figure out who they were or what they had been doing. After all, how many people try to climb into a leprosarium at 4:00 A.M. on a Sunday morning?

"Ma" Clinton looked at Margaret and Carrie across her cluttered desk. She didn't speak. She just stared at them. Margaret stared back. Finally, Kalihi's supervisor broke the impasse with a question.

"What did you do out there?"

"See one movie," Margaret answered. "Ate dinner and went to one dance at the Royal Hawaiian."

"Ma" Clinton had to struggle to keep from smiling when her thirteen-year-old leprosy patient blurted out that reply. But something in Margaret's eyes kept the compassionate woman from laughing. She knew how her patients were discriminated against. She had her own suspicions that most people were immune to the disease, but those suspicions would not be verified for twenty years. She also knew how crippling it was for the victims to be cut off from family and friends, locked away from normal social contact, and how liberating one Saturday night on the town might be for two young girls on their way to womanhood.

"All right, Margaret, Carrie, you are confined to your room, the cafeteria and classes for one week, and you cannot see this Friday's movie in the library."

"Ma" Clinton tried to sound firm, her sternest look upon her face. But "Ma" knew those library films were old, scratched and usually boring. The penalty was no penalty at all. As the girls turned to leave, "Ma" Clinton leaned across the desk and asked Margaret in a confidential whisper, "How was the movie?"

Margaret looked back towards "Ma" Clinton and whispered, "Oh. Very good. Miss Colbert's baby was cockaroached and one handsome man found 'im and brought 'im back."

With that, the conversation ended. Margaret and Carrie walked quickly from the room. Today, in the ghost-town ruins of Honolulu's Hale Mohalu hospital (the successor of the Kalihi Receiving Station), there is a plaque to Bessie "Ma" Clinton attached with brass screws to a large chunk of volcanic lava. It was salvaged from the ruins of the Kalihi Hospital and now stands among the rubble of this nation's recent history already forgotten. When she walked around the place, forty-five years after that morning session in "Ma" Clinton's office, Margaret looked down at the dusty monument and said, "She was one good lady."

It was "Ma" Clinton's dream that got a chapel built at the Kalihi Receiving Station. If her patients were to be cut off from the outside world, they would not be cut off from the church. So she began to scheme. When "Ma" asked the Health Board to fund the building of a chapel, they were sympathetic but had insufficient funds even to run the hospital adequately. Undaunted, she went to her staff and to her patients and they donated funds and labor to build it.

"We will have a place for my patients to worship God, to celebrate life and death," she said. And while Margaret was at Kalihi, sometime between 1934 and 1936, the chapel was dedicated to the "glory of God."

The church they built was approximately fifty feet long and thirty feet wide. When the pews were crowded, as they often were, the tiny chapel would hold about one hundred worshipers. Protestants and Catholics both took their turn. Margaret remembers, "We sang loud in that place. It was all wood, you know; it echoed all the way to King Street." When two patients fell in love, they were married inside. "Before," added Margaret, "when one patient die, his people may not care, you know. He just taken out and buried. Forgotten. Nobody there. But when we got our church, when patient die, all come with flowers, put 'em on casket and pray. He not alone anymore, 'cause "Ma" Clinton built us one church."

*   *   *

For millennia it was believed that leprosy caused hands, feet and faces to rot and drop away, leaving hideous deformity and life-long shame. Finally, the English surgeon, Dr. Paul Brand, working with leprosy victims in India with his wife, Dr. Margaret Brand, discovered that leprosy was a nerve disease that killed the victim's sense of pain. Leprosy didn't cause parts of the body to drop off. Rather, because the patient felt no pain, he might reach into hot coals to retrieve a fallen potato and burn himself seriously. Or, a victim might step on a rusty nail and again, because he felt no pain, continue to walk on that nail until a serious infection developed. Dr. Brand surprised the world with his discovery. It was those untreated burns, infections, ulcers and lacerations that caused the body to rot away, not leprosy. Those maladies could be treated even though leprosy was still without a sure cure. Faces, feet and hands could be saved. The hideous deformity and life-long shame could be remedied, at least in part.

Dr. Brand says that "the leprosy bacillus is a gentle, tolerant, almost friendly germ that can live in association with normal human cells without bothering them. They slowly mass and infiltrate. Victims can have billions of these enemy cells slowly thicken their skin without even feeling sick. They're just fellow travelers," he explains, "until the body senses them and begins to resent and resist the foreign proteins. Then the battle develops."

During her two and a half years at Kalihi, Margaret remembers how the skin on her hands and feet began to thicken as the bacilli grew in number. Though the doctors treated her, Margaret's condition worsened—often, she believes, because of the treatments, not in spite of them. She felt like a guinea pig in the underfunded and sometimes desperately experimental efforts to find the cause and cure of leprosy. She looks back at the long procession of doctors, nurses and lab technicians that treated her for forty years with mixed feelings, ranging from anger and horror to deepest respect and lifelong gratitude. Whatever their excesses, at Kalihi the doctors were trying to save this lovely teenager from the obviously growing ravages of her disease.

"In the dispensary they give us injections," she remembers. "Hundreds of little needles jabbing here and there. I get fever. Lie in bed many weeks. Suffer, you know. It hurt all the time."

Although the medical records are not available, doctors interviewed assume that Margaret's body was reacting negatively to the injections of chaulmoogra oil. When that process failed to control the nodules on her hands and feet, they tried another cure.

"My feet and hands came worse. My skin came bumpy, you know. Lots of lumps, swollen. My ear lobes came little bit longer. So they press my hands and feet in ice. They press ice on my ears. Ten, twenty times they press every day. Ice so cold it burns. Turn skin black. Still they press ice on nodules to burn them off and stop the spread. But it nevah work either."

Apparently, Margaret's doctors were treating her with dry ice or carbon dioxide snow to burn the bacilli with the freezing cold, hoping to kill them. This treatment was introduced to Kalihi about 1910 by Dr. J. T. Wayson. His young nephew continued experimenting with the treatment and might even have been Margaret's doctor. Carbon dioxide snow was applied to the area of the lesion or diseased area to dry it up. It helped many people. But Margaret felt embarrassed by the dark, black marks it left on her body, especially on her pretty legs; and as with many young patients, she would rather have the painful and embarrassing process stop, keep her legs their normal color, and live with her almost unnoticeable yet slowly spreading ailment.

"The one I don't like at all," Margaret adds, describing yet a third experiment, "was the electric one. They put wires around your hands. Then put the hands in one pan of water. Every day shock. Every day hands jump up and down. Still, my fingers bend until more and more like Mr. Albert's."

Electrical current was used to stimulate the flow of blood through Margaret's affected fingers. Doctors hoped the stimulated blood circulation would carry off the disease and begin healing Margaret's young hands before they, too, were bent and crippled like her teacher's. Nothing worked. Margaret's condition worsened. She remembers one visit, an especially painful visit by her father Charles.

Margaret's natural father stood outside the gate, waiting to see the young woman he had given away that stormy day fourteen years before. She ran down the lawn from the girls' building and stood happily smiling up at him through the wire-meshed fence. She greeted him and waited for the return greeting. He stared at her in shock. The nodules had thickened in her nose. Her hands and feet were plainly affected. But he had seen those changes before.

"What's a matta you stare at me?" Margaret asked, frightened by his silence.

Her father was a tall, handsome *haole* with a long, German nose and curly, brown hair. She was proud of the way he looked and wanted him to feel proud of the way she looked as well.

"Your eyebrow gone," he said, unbelieving. "Why they take it?"

Margaret's hand reached quickly to her face. Her left eyebrow was missing. Somehow, it had disappeared and she hadn't even noticed. She turned and ran to her room and looked in the mirror. She stared at her face, made lopsided by the missing eyebrow. In spite of all the painful treatments, the awful numbness of her disease was spreading. She could only continue the treatments even "if she no like" and hope that someday something would be found to arrest the disease at last.

Actually, Margaret had no choice. She was under age. She couldn't completely discontinue the treatments even if she wanted to. For her sister, Leilani, there was a choice. After childbirth, Leilani's initial swellings disappeared. Her soft, brown skin regained its initial texture. She refused to be jabbed, frozen and shocked. She refused to fight that quiet, camouflaged disease at work within her. The authorities begged her. Margaret begged her. Her parents begged her to take the treatments, but she refused. Shortly after she and Margaret arrived at the Kalihi Receiving Station, Leilani was sent to Kalaupapa, the leprosarium on Molokai. Margaret remained alone.

That aloneness was the most difficult part of her time at Kalihi. It wasn't the spreading disease nor the chaulmoogra oil injections, the icepacks or the electric shocks that the doctors prescribed to make her well. The most difficult part was what the law required of Margaret to keep the well from getting her disease. From the day she arrived at the Receiving Station, she was told that she could have no physical contact with healthy people inside or outside those high wire fences. Margaret could have visitors, but she could not touch them.

She loved those visits from her family. All four parents visited at least occasionally. But her natural mother, Edith, had diabetes and this illness, coupled with the embarrassment that she had turned Margaret in, kept her away. William worked most of the time and didn't really know what to say when he lined up with the other parents and tried to carry on a conversation with his teenage daughter. Charles, Margaret's natural father, and Ida, her second stepmother, came most often. Even when the

family came, they were not permitted to hug or hold or
even touch the increasingly lonely little girl. Nevertheless,
Margaret still remembers those occasional visits.

"My father, Charles, was one good German cook. He
used to make sauerkraut with hot dogs or with the head of
one pig, you know, German-kind things. He even cook me
chicken. He nevah like kill the chicken. Edith make him
kill 'em. Charles run around back yard chasing the bird.
The bird run under the house. Edith stay yelling from the
porch, 'Get the *moa*, you dumb German.' My father
more scared of Edith than the chicken, so he went catch
'em and wring the neck. He make chicken for me but he no
like.

"One time my mama, Ida, come see me.

"She say, 'You take your treatment today, baby?'

"I say, 'No, mama.'

"'Why you nevah take 'em?' she ask.

"'Because I no like!' I tell her.

"'Don't you evah talk to mama like that!' she say. 'I give
you dirty lickin'!'

"I laugh. One big fence stay between us now. She can't
give me lickin' less she climbs the fence, and I know she
nevah going climb that fence.

"'You nevah going give me no more lickin', mama. The
Lord take me away from you because you was very mean
to me. You can't be mean no more.'

"Then my mama start to cry. She take out one big
handkerchief. Blow her nose and say to me, 'I know, baby.
I no good. I treat you bad. I still worry. Forgive mama,
baby.'

"I forgive her again. Is easier to forgive mama than to
hate her. Then we stare at each other through the fence. I
start to cry. Mama nevah know what to say. She put her
hand on the fence. I want to take her hand but could not.
Then mama turn to go away. I want to yell, 'Come back,
mama. Hit me. Hug me. Anything. Just no go away,

mama. Please.' But I go back to room and nevah say nothing."

For almost three years, Margaret's treatment at Kalihi continued. The doctors and nurses, the lab technicians and administrative staff grew fond of the plucky, mixed-race kid with her sparkling eyes and sneaky, winsome ways. At their weekly medical review board meetings, her case was discussed again and again. One doctor would suggest a possible treatment. A lab technician would mention that her tests, though still positive, had shown some small signs of change. The nurses would report a blood count variation. Over and over, "Ma" Clinton would ask, "Can't we do anything?" Finally, the growing weight of evidence could no longer be denied. They voted that Margaret Kaupuni, the fourteen-year-old girl in Hoikiana, would be sent to Kalaupapa and her treatment continued there.

Margaret heard the quiet knock on her door and was surprised to find "Ma" Clinton standing in the doorway, a letter in her hand.

"May I come in, Margaret?"

"*Ae,*" the child answered, moving down the bed to give the older woman a place to sit. But Bessie Clinton wasn't in the mood for sitting.

"This is your letter from the Board of Health."

"Kalaupapa?" Margaret asked, knowing already what the letter meant. She remembered Leilani's letter. She had seen other patients at Kalihi get them including her friend Carrie. She knew what news the letter brought.

"Yes," "Ma" answered. "We will miss you."

Margaret doesn't remember feeling bad at all. She was going to a different place. It would be an interesting adventure. One island seemed no worse than another, even if it were the island of Damien, the island of death.

It was the rule that no healthy person touched a leprosy

patient. "Ma" Clinton enforced that rule with high fences
and clearly posted signs. But the day she left, "Ma"
Clinton, the chief of the Kalihi Station, leaned down,
kissed Margaret on the cheek and hugged her.

"*Aloha*, child. God go with you."

Above: A rare photo of the Kalawao side of the Kalaupapa Peninsula, the first home of leprosy victims isolated on Molokai. **Below:** Tourists stand on the *pali* [mountain] above the leprosarium on Molokai's Kalaupapa Peninsula. Now visitors ride mules on guided tours down the mountain to see the historic leprosarium (soon to be National Park), but in Margaret's day the *pali* separated her from the rest of Molokai and the world. (Photos courtesy of the State Archives of Hawaii.)

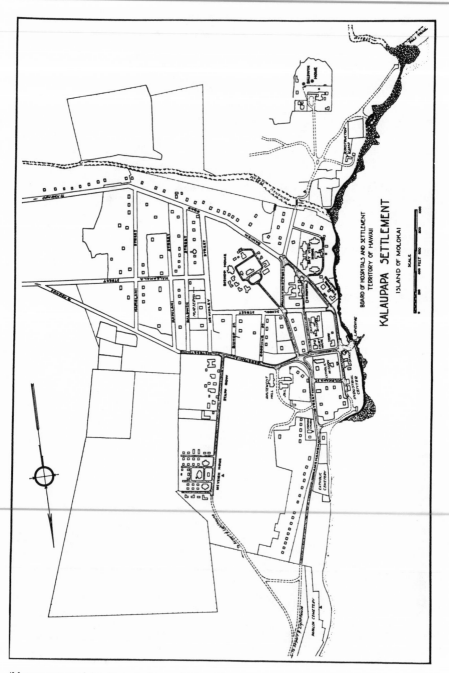

(Map courtesy of the State Archives of Hawaii.)

Above: An early photo of the Kalaupapa Leprosarium on Molokai. **Below:** The Bishop home, a residence for single female leprosy victims, was Margaret's first home at the leprosarium at Kalaupapa. (Photos courtesy of the State Archives of Hawaii.)

Above: Leprosy patients gathered around the empty grave of Father Damien. **Left:** A young leprosy victim poses with two priests at Kalaupapa's leprosarium. **Below:** Another rare Kalaupapa photo. (Photos courtesy of the State Archives of Hawaii.)

Above: Leprosy patients on Molokai waiting for treatment at the Kalaupapa Hospital. **Below:** A rare photo of a group of mourners around the casket of one of their fellow patients. Margaret remembers as many as six funerals a day during her early years at the island leprosarium. (Photos courtesy of the State Archives of Hawaii.)

Above: The leprosy patient band on Molokai. **Below:** A rare formal portrait of a group of leprosy patient girls from the Bishop Home on Molokai. (Photos courtesy of the State Archives of Hawaii.)

Mother Mary Jolenta, Mother Superior of the Franciscan nuns serving the patients of Kalaupapa's leprosarium when Margaret first arrived on Molokai. (Photo courtesy of the Honolulu *Star Bulletin*.)

"Mother" Alice and her flock of leprosy patients restored the historic Siloama Church and rediscovered the lost record book of the first congregation of Protestant Christians who were shipped to Molokai in 1866. (Photo courtesy of the Honolulu *Star Bulletin*.)

The Kanaana Hou Church on Kalaupapa, the Protestant church pastored by the Rev. Alice Kahokuoiuna. (Photo courtesy of the State Archives of Hawaii.)

Mamuli o ke Kauoha a ka Ahahui Luna
nakahiko o na Mokupuni o Maui, ma ko lakou
halawai ana ma Wailuku Maui i ka malama o
Okatoba M.H. 1866, ua hele ko lakou Komite, oia
o Rev A.O. Folepe a me Rev S.W. Nueku, a ua hiki
i Kalawao i Kahi o na mai Pake, ma ka la 23
o Dekemgba, M.H. 1866.

A no ka nele o na mai Pake, i ka Hale pule ole,
ia manawa, ua akoakoa mai lakou ma ka lanai
i o Ka Hale laau, Kahi i noho ai o Kapuhaia
    Malaila ua Kukulu ia Ka Ekalesia okoa o
na mai Pake, Malalo o ka malama ana, a
me ka hoomalu ana a ka Ahahui Lunakahiko
o na Mokupuni o Maui. A, elike hoi me ka hoo-
holo ana a ua Aha Lunakahiko la, ua noho o
Rev A.O. Folepe i Kuhu no ia ekalesia no kia
wa. Penei hoi ka hana o kela la,—
1 1, Ia Rev A.O. Folepe ka hai olelo imua o ke anaina
ma ka hoomaka ana, a ua kokua ia mai e
Rev S.W. Nueku mahope.
2 2. A, pau ia, Ua Ninaninau ia ka inoa
o na hoahanau e noho ana maglaila, a e hui
ana iloko oia ekalesia, He like me ka
mea i hoomaopopoia ma ka Aha olelo nui
o na Ekalesia ma Honolulu i hala aku, oia
hoi ka Halawai Makahiki o ka Aha Hui
Euanerio o ko Hawaii Pae Aina ma Honolulu i
June M.H. 1866, ua hookuu ia mai keia mau
hoahanau mai ko lakou mau Ekalesia mai
e hui pu i Ekalesia okoa ma Kalawao Molokai. He 35 ka huina o na hoahanau, e loaa
na inoa oia poe hoahanau ma ka Papa inoa i
kakau ia ma ka aoao 22 a hiki i ka aoao —
keia Buke,)
    Ua heluhelu ia ke Kahua o ka manao
a me ka Bepita o ka Ekalesia i hoopukaia
e ka Ahahui Lunakahiko o na Mokupuni
o Maui, ma ko lakou "Buke Law Lima"
ana ae mai "me ka hoohiki pu no hoi", na
hoahanau, Alaila, ua hoomaikai ia kela
hana me ka pule.
3   Alaila, ua koho ia e na hoahanau
akah mau Kanaka o lakou i mau Luna

Page one of the Siloama Church Record Book. Written in beautiful Hawaiian script, it describes the history of the first Protestant congregation of leprosy victims on Molokai. (Photo reproduced by permission of the Hawaiian Mission Children's Society.)

III.

LEPROSARIUM
ON
MOLOKAI

1936–69

The half-hearse, half-passenger bus from Kalihi Station turned left off Fort Street onto Ala Moana Boulevard. One passenger-patient looked up at the 'Aloha Tower' and began to weep quietly. The vehicle jogged right into a parking area near the main docks of Honolulu Harbor and stopped in the shadow of the old steamship, *Hawaii*. A small crowd of parents and friends, reflecting various stages of grief, anger or disbelief, stood behind a wooden barricade near the passenger boarding ramp. The patients bound for Molokai's leprosarium climbed out of their transport. They stood stoically in line with only an occasional timid wave or embarrassed smile at family and friends who had come to say good-bye. Fourteen-year-old Margaret climbed down last, carrying a gray cardboard suitcase only partially filled with her few treasured belongings collected during two and one-half years at the Kalihi Hospital.

Charles Frederick stood alone and apart from the others in that crowd behind the barricade. Margaret's natural father watched his *hānai* [given away for adoption] daughter take her place in the line of people about to sail away into exile. Her young body still showed few signs of disease. She looked so small and lonely to her father. He longed to call her name, but he could say nothing. He remembered feeling the same awful, silent grief fourteen years earlier when he had given Margaret to Moriah and William.

Margaret's stepmother, Ida, was also alone in the crowd that day. William had stayed in their small apartment in Moiliili, made too ill by his anger and helplessness to say good-bye. As Margaret got in line with the other leprosy patients, Ida pushed her way through the crowd, grasped the wood slat wall that separated them and began to cry.

"Margaret! Margaret!"

Margaret noticed her stepmother leaning against the barricade and wondered why she was crying. The child was excited, happily anticipating her first boat ride, eager to visit another island. In her last visit to the Kalihi hospital, Ida had wailed in the same way. "No go dat place," she had warned her child. "You going *make* [die] ovah there and nevah come back."

Margaret looked over the two wooden walls that made a path between them across the wharf and up the boarding gangplank.

"No cry, Mama," she shouted, "I like go different place. No worry."

Ida only cried louder. Margaret turned away, distracted by the cacophony of strange new sights and sounds. The noise was deafening. Winches whirred and strained to haul netted cargo up on deck. Sweating Hawaiian stevedores swore and railed against the barrels they were rolling into the ship's rapidly filling holds. In the hot sun, trucks waiting to unload their easily spoiled produce honked for attention. Above the din the ship's steam-siren sounded impatiently. Suddenly, a small herd of cattle pounded from their holding pens in a nearby warehouse, thundered down the narrow fence channel between Margaret and Ida and up into the restraining pens on the rear deck of the ship.

The line of leprosy patients followed the cattle on board and were penned up near them on the open deck. Margaret stood on a little wooden bench and waved down at Ida as the ship pulled away from the dock into the busy harbor on Mamal Bay. The crowd disappeared, Ida with them, still weeping. Charles Frederick stood alone on the wharf and watched the *Hawaii* until it steamed over the horizon and disappeared, a tiny fleck of sadness on the open sea.

Another name for leprosy in the musical and poetic tongue of Hawaii is *ma'i-ho'oka'awale 'ohana*, the disease-that-tears-families-apart. For sixty-eight years, since 1866, families had gathered at Honolulu Harbor as they gathered that day to watch their afflicted loved ones carried away to the island of Molokai's Kalaupapa Leprosarium. Since ancient times, lepers have been treated differently than victims of any other disease. For thousands of years they were segregated from society, isolated, cast out into the deserts or mountains, onto islands or into compounds with guards and tall fences. In the Middle Ages, people with leprosy were imprisoned in Lazar Houses (House of Lazarus) and called "unclean." They were kept out of contact with society to stop the spread of the disease and to keep people who did not have the disease from being inconvenienced and horrified by the suffering of leprosy victims. Strict rules were made and enforced to keep those who had leprosy from marrying or having children so that blood lines that "bred" the illness would be destroyed. In some societies, people with leprosy were simply murdered, their infected bodies burned and buried.

Now we know that practically all adults and most children are immune to the disease. Now we know that leprosy can be arrested and cured. Now we know that a patient under treatment by the modern sulfone drugs is not infectious, even if he still carries bacteria of the disease in his body, and that most victims can be treated as out-patients in a regular hospital or clinic. Now we know, too, that people's fear of being isolated kept them from reporting symptoms of the disease and getting those symptoms diagnosed and treated. But less than fifty years ago, when Margaret was sent to Molokai, almost nothing was known of the cause or spread of leprosy, and so, another teenage girl was banished from her home and family to an isolated island peninsula where she would live for more than three decades.

Margaret remembers that her first boat ride turned out to be no interisland pleasure cruise. "They ship us with the cattle," she recalls. "We out on deck. Many hours. Very hot. So hot. Finally, they put up canvas ovahhead. Then sea get very rough. I get sick and sick. Finally, night time, we arrive Kalaupapa, Molokai."

The island of Molokai is twenty-five miles due east of Oahu. Against the strong wind and heavy sea currents, the steamship covered that distance in just over seven hours. In the yellow light of sunset, Margaret could barely make out the almost half-mile high cliffs that separated the tiny island peninsula from the rest of Molokai. The peninsula of Kalaupapa is on the north central side of Molokai. It is about 6,630 acres (only 10 square miles of the island's 260-square-mile surface) in the shape of a pointed leaf surrounded on three sides by the ocean and backed by the high mountain cliffs. In the center of the peninsula is one small volcanic crater, Kauhako, only 405 feet high. In the bottom of the crater, the sea surges with the tide. Kalaupapa Town lies on the southern base of the peninsula where the *pali* [mountain] and the peninsula intersect.

By the time the leprosy victims and their supplies were loaded on the whale boat that would take them into the harbor, darkness had fallen and the lights of Kalaupapa Town shimmered out across the water. Margaret stared unbelieving at the crowd above her on the wharf as the bright loading light was turned on and friendly hands reached down to help her disembark. Most of the 500 patients had gathered to welcome the newcomers. She stared up at them from the boat, cringing behind a bale of produce to avoid their helping hands.

In the bright light flickering off the water, her fellow victims' deformities were eerily displayed. They were in far worse condition than any leprosy patients she had seen at Kalihi Hospital. A choir of faces smiled their strangely bloated, cockeyed smiles down at her from the pier above. The twisted hands that finally helped her to the dock were far more clawlike than Mr. Albert's had been. Some had almost no hands at all, just ugly bloated stumps.

As Margaret stumbled along the wharf, still clutching her gray cardboard suitcase, the patients hobbled up to her on toeless, stunted feet to wish her welcome. Ear lobes hung down almost shoulder length, stretched and twisted by the disease. Heads tilted awkwardly so that half-out-of-socket eyeballs could see her. Other eyes stared unseeing and unblinking as she passed. Little kerchiefs fluttered at hundreds of throats covering tracheotomy tubes through which the victims breathed. Patients without faces talked through open holes in red, disfigured flesh. Rough, raw welts covered elephantine arms and legs, chests and backs. Strange raspy voices welcomed her.

"Hi, girl." . . . "Welcome Molokai." . . . "You Leilani's little sister? She say you come today."

Margaret tried to avoid the offered hands and outstretched arms of Kalaupapa.

"Oh," she said, backing away, "please not touch."

Then someone called her name.

"Margaret, don't do that."

Margaret whirled, "Leilani!" The little girl dropped her cardboard case and ran into the arms of the sister she hadn't seen since they were separated at the Kalihi Receiving Station.

"Touch them, Margaret, or they going be hurt."

Margaret clutched her sister tightly and refused to even look at the people crowding in.

"I no like hurt nobody. I no want nobody for touch me either." Margaret began to cry. The patients stood back, embarrassed by her tears. They remembered when they too had landed at Kalaupapa. They remembered when they too had cried tears of fear and tears of self-pity.

Leilani led her sister from the wharf onto Beretania Street past the Catholic Mission, the community store and Kalawao County's little courthouse. They turned right on Kamehameha Street, walked past the Calvinist Mission and up School Street to the tall white gates of the Bishop Home for Women and Girls. At the front porch of the Main House, a tall nun stood in full black habit and wimple to greet her.

"This Mother Mary Jolenta," said Leilani. "She take care of you now."

Leilani turned and ran back down the path toward town.

"Where you going, Leilani?" Margaret called after her, afraid to be left alone again.

Leilani stopped and stared at her sister, then up at the hovering, unsmiling nun. She knew it wasn't the time or place to tell Margaret about Mother Marianne's grave and the boy who waited for her there. Margaret would learn the ropes for herself soon enough.

"I be back, Margaret. Mother Jolenta going take good care you."

With that, Leilani whirled and ran back down the sloping grass hillside toward the sea.

"Come, child. You must be very hungry after your voyage. We've saved dinner for you."

Margaret followed the tall nun in her heavy woolen robe into the cafeteria. The tables were already set with brown crockery bowls and matching mugs for breakfast. Margaret was very hungry. On the ship she had tried to eat the box lunch from Kalihi Receiving Station but the sandwiches were soggy and she was terribly seasick. This would be her first real meal of the day.

"Here, girl. Eat dis bread. We bake."

Margaret looked up, startled, as an older woman patient set down a plate of bread on the table before her. The patient's hands were both bandaged. The gauze and tape were soaked with a red, pus-like fluid, draining from the covered sores. Margaret stared at the wet bandaged fingers that lifted the bread from its plate into Margaret's bowl.

"I not hungry," Margaret said, turning away.

"Maybe you like hot chocolate," the patient asked, obviously concerned about the frightened young girl's appetite. "Taste good!"

Margaret stared at the patient's disfigured face and nodded in silent assent.

The woman hurried away and returned almost immediately with a cup of steaming chocolate. Her unfeeling fingers clutched the cup by its rim. Ooozing, blood-red fingertips dipped accidentally into the chocolate. Margaret felt sick. The patient smiled down at her a twisted, loving smile.

"Drink. Good for you."

"Thank you, Mrs. Paka."

The nun dismissed the motherly patient and set down a large bowl of soup and a plate of crackers before Margaret. Margaret ate what the nun served, then followed her to the patient's quarters in Bungalow B nearby.

There were six other young women in Margaret's bungalow. They looked almost normal to the new arrival. Apparently, the disease was still in its early stages in them, too. The overpowering sense of decay and death that Margaret felt on the wharf and in the cafeteria was noticeably absent there. Suddenly, the quiet in the bungalow was broken by the loud rhythms of the *Kā'eke'eke* hula. Margaret spun around to find Carrie, her young friend from the Kalihi Receiving Station, playing two broom handles against a wooden bunkbed.

"Carrie!" Margaret screamed with delight and ran to embrace her friend.

"Margaret!" Carrie screamed back. "You still dance at Royal Hawaiian?"

Carrie told the story of their escape from the Kalihi Hospital and that one grand night on the town. She told how Margaret planned to avoid capture by threatening to spread leprosy up and down Waikiki. The girls howled with laughter. During the story, a bell sounded. The lights switched off. The women's voices automatically dropped to a whisper.

"It's Mother Jolenta," Carrie explained. "We go sleep every night at ten o'clock or we work so long time in kitchen."

The young women groaned quietly. Margaret undressed in the semidarkness and climbed into bed. For a while, she listened to their voices. She said nothing; she couldn't. Her lips trembled still from the excitement and the terror of her arrival on Molokai. She couldn't close her eyes tight enough to block out the memories of those crippled bodies at the wharf. In the stillness, Margaret wondered if she would look as bad as they one day.

Her open palms traveled nervously back and forth over the rough sheets. She tried to stretch her hands completely flat against the iron bed, but already muscles were wasting away. Fingers were slowly curling in and could not be fully straightened no matter how hard Margaret tried. In the darkness, she could feel the slightly thickening flesh upon her hands and feet. Her face felt normal except for the missing eyebrow. There were some first signs of leprous nodules forming in her nose.

Sensing her friend's loneliness, Carrie whispered, "Hey, Margaret, tomorrow we . . ."

But Carrie stopped mid-sentence when a tall shadow appeared at the window and a slender shadow-hand tapped gently on the window pane.

"Kalaupapa Prison," a patient whispered.

"Sergeant Jolenta on guard duty," another patient replied.

"Shut up, lepers," a third patient mocked, "you need beauty rest or you going get real ugly."

"Just like Jolenta," whispered Carrie.

The girls laughed. The shadow-hand tapped again. This time the girls sensed its final warning and their whispering stopped in unison. The shadow listened for the silence; then, slowly, Mother Mary Jolenta walked from Bungalow B across the Bishop Home grounds to the little chapel in the nunnery.

Twelve Franciscan nuns were waiting in the small room with its candle-lit altar and hand embroidered kneeling pillows. When Mother Jolenta, the Mother Superior on Kalaupapa entered the room, the sisters stood, bowed courteously, opened their Latin breviarys and knelt to begin night prayers. In a firm but musical voice, Mother Jolenta officiated throughout the service. Margaret lay on her bed near an open window and could hear the sisters sing their evening prayers.

"The Lord Almighty grant us a peaceful night and a perfect end."

"Amen," the sisters answered and knelt to pray.

In 1882, fifty-two years before, King Kalakaua commissioned a young Catholic priest to find an order of nuns who would risk their lives to serve the suffering leprosy victims in Hawaii. Father Leonore traveled across the United States appealing to convent after convent seeking committed women for the task. He visited fifty missions, all too understaffed and overworked to accept the challenge. Then, in the Franciscan Convent of St. Anthony of Syracuse, New York, twenty-four sisters volunteered and six were spared for the work in Hawaii.

"Our help is in the name of the Lord," affirmed Mother Jolenta.
"The maker of heaven and of earth," answered the nuns.

On October 22, 1883, the Reverend Mother Marianne, provincial of the Franciscan Motherhouse in Syracuse, led her six young companions up the gangplank of the steamer Mariposa and eighteen days later, November 8, 1883, they rounded Diamond Head and landed in Honolulu Harbor. A pilot boat flying the royal colors sped to shore bearing the news to an exuberant King Kalakaua that the brave young nuns had landed. Four royal carriages carried the startled sisters through the streets. Bèlls rang out the news. Cheering Hawaiians greeted them. A public service of Thanksgiving was held in the Cathedral. On a visit later that day to greet the sisters, Queen Kapiolani, tears streaming down her face, said to the nuns from Syracuse, "I love you. You have left your home and friends to come to these faraway islands to care for my afflicted children. I shall never forget you—you are my own sisters."

"In you, Lord, have I taken refuge," sang Mother Jolenta.
"In you, Lord, have we put our trust," sang the nuns.

Almost immediately the cheering crowds left Mother Marianne and her six companions with their first task: salvaging the primitive Kakaako Branch Hospital where leprosy patients were isolated near Honolulu before being shipped to Molokai. The sisters found Kakaako's facilities continually flooded by the sea. There was little if any treatment for the bodies or the souls of the miserable victims. The sisters moved onto the grounds. Mother Marianne took charge of the dispensary. The nuns dressed the patients' sores; the presence of these brave young women among the hideously deformed gave the victims of leprosy new hope and new self-respect.

When the women discovered that children born of leprous patients on Molokai were exposed to the physical and moral dangers of that settlement, Mother Marianne and Queen Kapiolani founded the Kapiolani Children's Home to provide a place of care for the patients' children. Mother Marianne planned to accompany her sisters to Hawaii to see them settled and then return to New York. After five years of working with the leprosy patients on Oahu, news came from Molokai that Father Damien, himself afflicted with leprosy, was dying. Mother Marianne convinced the authorities that she and her sisters should be allowed to move into a bungalow at the newly built Bishop Home at Kalaupapa to better serve the patients there. In 1888, Mother Marianne sailed for Molokai. She never returned to Syracuse; she was buried forty years later on Kalaupapa.

"We praise you, Father, for your gifts," sang the nuns.
"Of dusk and nightfall over earth,
"Foreshadowing the mystery
"Of death that leads to endless day."

Mother Jolenta and her sisters followed Mother Marianne by almost fifty years. Still, they wore the heavy wool habits and tall white wimples of the Franciscans. Still, they began and ended each day with hymns of praise and prayers for themselves and their patients. And still, they refused to compromise the disciplines that brought new life to them and to the suffering people they served.

The girls in Margaret's bungalow had no idea what it had taken in courage for those first nuns (or for those who followed fifty years later) to land and wade ashore onto that stormy peninsula; to help establish order where all too often there was anarchy; to protect the women patients from men who, drunk and hopeless, would terrorize them; to love and cajole a people who had given up hoping to learn new vocations, to continue their painful and often

futile treatments and to plan their future in spite of the
death that grew within them.

Robert Louis Stevenson visited Mother Marianne and
wrote:

> To see the infinite pity of this place,
> The mangled limb, the devastated face.
> The innocent sufferer smiling at the rod;
> A fool were tempted to deny his God.
>
> He sees and shrinks but if he look again
> Lo, beauty springing from the breast of pain
> He marks the sisters on the painful shores
> And even a fool is silent and adores.

Mother Jolenta and her sisters closed their night prayers
in unison:

*"Protect us, Lord, as we stay awake; watch over us as
we sleep, that awake, we may keep watch with Christ, and
asleep, rest in his peace. Amen."*

Then there was silence. Margaret could hear the sisters'
quiet steps as they walked from the chapel to their simple
quarters in silent meditation. Once more, Mother Jolenta's
shadow paused, then passed. This time Margaret felt
comforted by that stern, yet loving presence.

Margaret awakened at sunrise to the voices of Mother
Jolenta and the nuns singing:

> O God our help in ages past
> Our hope for years to come.
> Our shelter from the stormy blast,
> And our eternal home.

Her new friends in Bungalow B were groaning awake.
"How dey can sing befoa breakfast?" somebody asked.

"How dey can sing afta breakfast?" a second girl answered. "One moa runny egg and I going *kau kau* [kill and eat] da chicken."

"No forget your boots, girls," chimed in a third. "Today taro day."

The girls groaned through shower line and through their breakfast of rice and fruit, eggs and milk. They groaned on their way to Kalaupapa's wharf and they groaned when on the horizon appeared the little interisland steamer with its weekly load of taro root. Carrie took Margaret to the meathouse near the wharf where large vats of water were boiling and clusters of women patients were pulling on boots and rubber gloves. Carrie showed Margaret how to sign in with the patient foreman and take her place in the group of women waiting for the work day to begin.

Taro root looks like a clump of mixed-size Irish potatoes and is native to the Pacific Islands. It is boiled, peeled and mashed into poi, a favorite island food. Margaret learned to make poi during Ida's year as an invalid. Then, she bought and boiled one or two taro roots, but to see that ship unload hundreds of pounds of root and to anticipate peeling and pounding all that poi was really quite overwhelming to the fourteen-year-old newcomer.

Women dumped boxes of taro into the steaming cauldrons. Other women fished out the boiled roots and hauled them to the waiting workers. Each woman carried sharpened fish bone or opihi shell (the sea urchin shaped like a Chinese coolie's hat with sharp fluted edges). Workers scraped off the outer shell of the taro with their native tools. Other workers mashed and pounded and strained the taro into poi. Margaret remembers that as they worked, the women talked mainly about the men of Kalaupapa.

"You pretty Margaret. You going get da best."

"*Ae*," a middle-aged woman added, "but no go Mother Marianne's grave too soon. It won't be ghost dat gets you there."

The women giggled. Carrie whispered to Margaret that

Mother Marianne was buried in a shady grove of trees behind the social hall. Young men patients who lived in the very unprivate dormitories of Baldwin Home liked to use that convenient spot to court the girls of Kalaupapa.

By midday, temperatures inside the humid meathouse reached over 100 degrees. The women worked and sweat and giggled as they produced the leprosarium's weekly supply of poi. (For this, Margaret would receive six dollars a week in spending money on Kalaupapa. The government supplied clothes, room, board, treatment. Those six dollars were for incidentals, especially beer.) Margaret enjoyed the attention the older women showed her, the advice they freely gave.

Later that day, Leilani found Margaret with her new friends, soaking their feet in the Pacific near the meathouse.

"Margaret, come! We going visit uncle now."

Margaret remembered well her natural mother Edith's younger brother, George. He was a handsome Hawaiian who lived in a funny, hand-made wooden shack at Laea Bay on the north shore of Oahu. George only worked in the sugar mill near Kahuku when he ran out of money to buy beer or pork for *laulau* [a chopped taro leaf, fish, pork and chicken mixture wrapped in a ti plant leaf and steamed in the sand]. George loved the sea. When he wasn't netfishing the coral reefs in Laea Bay or surfing Waimea, he was sitting in the rusty ruins of his vintage Ford, staring out to sea.

On several very special occasions, Edith had taken Margaret on the North Shore bus to visit her uncle. George taught the little girl to swim. She still remembered how he ran down the beach and somersaulted into the surf. She loved riding in front of him on his long hollow surfboard. George told her stories of the sea, of the white *manō* [shark] or the *kākū* [barracuda] that could unlock his jaw to swallow fish twice the size of his mouth and of the *pūhi* [eel] who would bite the end of the *haoa pūhi* [eel catching stick] and hold on until he died. Margaret still remembered how proud she felt walking alongside her handsome young uncle as the *haole* tourist ladies smiled up at them.

Leilani led her little sister through Kalaupapa Settlement up Kaleakala Street to a little rough wood framed cottage overlooking the Pacific. Margaret could see her uncle silhouetted against the sun staring out to sea. It would be good to feel his strong hands lift her once again and hold her up against the sky. He would call her by her Hawaiian name, Makalika, she was sure of that, and he would tell her how she had grown in these past five years.

"Give your uncle a kiss," whispered Leilani.

"*Makua kāne* [Uncle]!" Margaret cried, running towards the silhouetted figure.

The man in the wheel chair turned and smiled. "Makalika!"

Margaret took one look at the horribly deformed face, scaly skin and clawlike hands of her uncle, turned and ran to her sister crying.

"Don't do that!" Leilani scolded. "He going feel hurt!"

Margaret cried hysterically and threw herself onto her sister, refusing to look again at the man who used to run along beside her in the sand. She sobbed both from horror and from shame. In that awkward moment, George turned his chair and wheeled up to the girls.

"Leilani, no make her kiss me. She cannot help. First time she see dis kind *ma'i-Pākē* [leprosy]."

Margaret knew that gentle voice and slowly turned to look down at him. His ear lobes hung down to his shoulders. One eyeball barely balanced in its socket. His face resembled shapeless putty, twisted by demonic hands. His back was stooped and covered with red welts. One foot had been amputated. In five short years, the final stages of lepromatous leprosy had come out of hiding, weakened and destroyed the young man she idolized.

Margaret remembers how she turned away from her

uncle and her sister and ran down the hill toward Bishop
Home. "It's O.K., Makalika," her uncle shouted after her,
"you come back visit uncle when you ready."

In her hurry to escape, Margaret missed the turn down
Kaleakala Street and for awhile wandered through the
married patient neighborhood above the bay. During that
pleasant hour before sunset patients were working in their
yards or sipping beer on their porches. Now Margaret
compares that first lonely tour of Kalaupapa to a long walk
through a circus freak show. The patients smiled and
waved at her but she tried not to notice them, walking face
down straight ahead hoping she would find Carrie or the
Bishop Home before she broke down and cried again.

As she passed a little building marked Kalaupapa Jail, a
group of young men patients carrying a volleyball net
passed her.

"Hi, girl," one called.

"Hey, Wiley, she *keiki* [child]," his friend chided him.

"Don't rob da cradle!" added a third.

"Shut up, Loo," the young man responded. The boys
laughed and continued on toward Baldwin Home, but the
first boy stood in the road, still smiling at Margaret.

"Come on, Wiley. We go."

Wiley let his friends walk on without him and then
moved slowly towards Margaret. She noticed his hands,
like hers, were only slightly bent. His mouth, too, was
slightly affected by the disease. But there were no other
obvious signs of leprosy on the young man.

"You came last night," he said. "I saw you at da wharf."

Margaret backed away. "Ya, I come last night, but I
nevah see you. Now I going find Carrie. Bye."

Margaret turned and walked down Beretania, away
from Bishop Home towards the center of town.

"Carrie Haruko?" Wiley asked. Margaret nodded.

"You no find her there. Carrie stay Bishop Home. Come,
I show you."

Wiley took Margaret's arm and led her past the hospital
and up the road to Bishop Home.

"I Wiley Kihe. What your name?"

"I Margaret Kaupuni," she answered.

He smiled at her as she turned and ran away from him up toward Bishop.

"Bye, Margaret Kaupuni. Friday night you come da movie with me."

Margaret heard his invitation but did not look back. That Friday night, however, Wiley Kihe, a nineteen-year-old from Kona, Hawaii, with tuberculoid leprosy, escorted fourteen-year-old Margaret Kaupuni to the Social Hall at Kalaupapa. They watched Frederick March in his 1932 Academy Award winning portrayal of *Dr. Jekyll and Mr. Hyde.* The badly scratched and jumpy 16-mm movie print only enhanced the scariness of the film for Margaret. Most of the other patients laughed and whispered as handsome Dr. Jekyll was transformed by false teeth, putty nose, hairy gorilla hands and makeup into a monster who frightened no one else in that audience of leprosy victims.

Soon after Margaret's arrival on Molokai, the entire Kalaupapa Settlement turned out to greet another shipload of newcomers to the island. This time the steamer was draped in colorful nautical pennants, the red, blue and white of Hawaii and the scarlet, black and gold of Belgium. A fleet of small boats was lowered to carry an obviously important group of passengers to shore. None were patients.

Carrie and Margaret were just leaving the village store after deliciously squandering their paycheck on goodies thought appropriate by the two fourteen-year-old shoppers when Carrie saw the crowd at the wharf and ran to join them. Margaret, still frightened by the sight of the more deformed patients, stood away from the crowd on an outcropping of rock below the visitors' quarters.

Dr. Tuttle was there, and Father Peter and Mother Jolenta with her nuns and Pastor Koni and the administrative staff all lined up wearing official smiles of greeting. Even from a distance, Margaret could see Dr. Tuttle place the traditional bright orange Kikania lei around the clergyman dressed entirely in black. The patients did not join in greeting. They stood quietly as the Bishop from Europe and his party of dignitaries were led through their midst to the visitors' quarters. The European clerics smiled and nodded pleasantly at the patients but the patients stared back in silence. Carrie spotted Margaret and scrambled down the rocks to share the gossip.

"They here to take Damien away," she said. "Nobody happy, not even Mother Jolenta."

Margaret looked confused.

"Who is Damien?" she asked, her mouth still full of sticky rice candy.

"He was one big priest here. Dead and buried over Kalawao side. They going dig him up and take him home. Everybody stay real mad. Come!"

By the time the girls had finished dinner, they had discovered why the people of Kalaupapa were so angry. Father Damien de Veuster, a missionary priest from Tremeloo, Belgium, had given his life in service to the leprosy patients on Molokai. During his sixteen years on the island peninsula (1873–1889) Damien had contracted the disease and was buried with those he served in a small graveyard beside his church. The King of Belgium had written President Roosevelt requesting that the Territory of Hawaii grant Belgium the privilege of honoring its native son for his exemplary service to God and to mankind. The young bishop Margaret had seen disembark at the head of a delegation of European and Hawaiian dignitaries had come to exhume the body of Molokai's legendary priest. The man who had loved the victims of leprosy and died in their midst was about to be taken from them forever.

"No good," an old woman muttered to the girls. "*Kapu* [taboo]," she whispered.

Other patients nodded in agreement.

"Somebody going die when da grave of dis great man disturb."

Margaret watched the old women whisper the ancient Hawaiian curse and wondered why one dead priest could be so important to the people of his far-off country or to the people of her new island home.

The ancient Egyptians called leprosy the death before death. The Old Testament Hebrew writers described leprosy as an expression of God's punishment upon its victim. Moses instructed his people that the persons afflicted "be cast out of the camp of the children of Israel." "All the days wherein the plague is in him, he shall be unclean; he is unclean: he shall dwell alone; without the camp shall his dwelling be" (Lev. 13:46).

Because there was no known cure for the disease, it became standard practice for ancient civilizations to cast out the victim from his home and village. Still, leprosy spread. By the twelfth and thirteenth centuries, leprosy had affected an estimated one-fourth of the entire population of northern Europe. In their attempt to eliminate this plague, Old Testament instructions were carefully followed by the church. Once a victim's leprosy was established by a local physician, a priest was called to perform last rites and to hold a funeral mass for the victim bearing the living death in his body.

Before the funeral mass, the victim was reminded that leprosy was his punishment from God and that he could not escape that punishment. During the funeral mass, instead of a casket, a black canopy was built before the altar and the leprosy victim sat behind it, hearing family and friends mourn his passing. The rite continued at the graveyard where, before a freshly dug grave, the priest threw a symbolic handful of dirt upon the victim reminding all of his death. From that moment, he was dead to family and friends. Even his property was distributed to his heirs. The victim was forced to travel the land carrying a bell or rattle and warning all who passed that he was "unclean."

Driven from city to city, the leprosy victim was hated or feared by all he met.

Damien was not the first priest (or layperson) to serve the persons afflicted with leprosy. From the same church that cast out the leprosy victim came brave men and women to give them comfort and solace on their lonely journey. (For example, in the Middle Ages the Lazar houses, almost 2,000 of them, were places of care and refuge founded by brave priests and nuns in Europe to serve the outcast.) But unlike those others who served and died, unknown and unpraised, Damien's life and death sparked the public's curiosity.

Damien, although himself a poor man, left the comforts of Europe and eventually became an outcast with the outcasts. While serving the leprosy settlement on Molokai, he disobeyed all the traditional rules and even let those with leprosy eat from his plate, drink from his glass and smoke his pipe. As God became a man to win men, explained Damien, so he lived like those afflicted with leprosy to prove God's love to them in his own body.

The story of this young priest standing one eventful day before his congregation in St. Philomina Church and announcing, "WE who are lepers," moved and fascinated the entire world. Forty-six years after his death, his story told and retold by such able advocates as Robert Louis Stevenson and John Farrow, Damien became a legend and the people of Belgium wanted the body of their legend back.

Though uncertain why the settlement would make such a fuss over the body of a priest, Margaret joined the long procession of patients on their two-and-one-half-mile trek from the Kalaupapa side of the peninsula to Kalawao, the old site of the first leprosarium on Molokai. Patients piled into the few cars and trucks on the island, rode horseback or walked the distance carrying food and beer and a few *'upena kiloi* [throwing nets] to catch fish for the afternoon meal. For Margaret it was a day off, a celebration, a picnic; but most of the marchers in that long parade were sullen and silent on the long walk across the peninsula to Kalawao Town. Nearing the old settlement site the road was pressed on both sides by a jungle of ferns, vines, native bushes and trees.

The patients gathered near St. Philomena's, the old square-towered stone church erected by Damien and his patients. The sound of pick and shovel echoed from Kalawao cemetery to the nearby *pali* and back to the patients watching in silence. As the casket was removed from the crypt, the patients began to weep and mutter angrily. John Farrow reports that the young bishop in his formal black vestments and purple biretta told the patients, "We have heard your protest and sympathize with your opposition to his removal from your midst, but today his native country, which gave him to us, claims him. His country desires to bestow upon him honors which cannot be given in this remote island spot." The mourners filed by the open casket paying their last farewell; then, as the body was driven away, they joined in singing the islands' plaintive song of good-bye, *"Aloha Oe."*

Weeks later, the patients on Kalaupapa were not surprised to learn that the captain of the steamer carrying Damien's body to its final burial in Belgium disappeared from the bridge of his ship and was never seen again. Upon hearing the news, the patients agreed that the curse had its victim. The empty grave of Damien had been avenged.

Margaret soon adjusted to the new routines in her life on Kalaupapa. There was breakfast at the Bishop Home with Mother Jolenta and her nuns always hovering nearby. She took her daily turn preparing meals, setting table or washing dirty dishes. The work days were spent scraping taro root to make poi or washing sheets and towels in the settlement's hot, noisy laundry. In the evening she joined Carrie and her new friends to watch the younger men play volleyball, baseball or badminton. She still remembers how well the men played with their crippled, clawlike hands, stumped feet, bent and often twisted bodies. After the games, the crowd stopped by Tomita's store for beer and conversation. Though curfew was early, the more daring couples would do their courting on the beach or in the grove of trees hiding Mother Marianne's grave from prying eyes.

On Saturdays, Margaret would line up in Kalaupapa's little hospital with the other out-patients for weekly doses of chaulmoogra oil. She remembers drinking the thick, nauseous oil from the capsules and rubbing it into her skin everyday hoping the gooey mass would surround and destroy the leprous bacilli growing there. When Dr. Hirschey or Dr. Tuttle came from Oahu to examine and treat the patients, they continued to press carbon dioxide snow on Margaret's more advanced concentrations of leprosy hoping to burn back and kill the bacilli. As the nodules growing inside Margaret's nose thickened and impaired her breathing, the doctors tried to burn a hole through the congested nasal passages with a needle-shaped electric instrument coated with silver nitrate. With every visit to the hospital, Margaret felt her leprosy worsen rather than improve. But she remembered "Ma" Clinton's words: "We can only help you if you take your medicine and treatments every day, even if you 'no like.'" Margaret didn't like the treatments, but she refused to quit fighting her disease as had so many patients at Kalaupapa.

On Saturdays there were beach excursions to watch the men fish with 'upena kiloi [a throwing net weighted around the exterior line with lead weights], to wade in the tide pools in search of 'opihi urchins, or to hike down the side of the volcanic crater to the lake at the bottom where the sea surged noisily with each changing tide. Saturday night there were scratchy old movies that seldom got through a showing without breaking down, or dances at Paschoal Hall. Patients and nonpatients alike were invited to the dances, but because patients and nonpatients were not to have any physical contact, the dance floor was divided down the center. Often enterprising nonpatients would steal bandages from the hospital and disguise themselves as patients in order to dance with a patient friend. Saturday nights, too, after long walks in the moonlight or times of courting in the thick grove of trees near Mother Marianne's grave, there was the quick dash past the waiting nuns at Bishop Home who stayed vigilant on their Saturday night detail until every bed was occupied, every girl safe away from the boys of Baldwin Home.

On Sunday mornings there was Catholic, Protestant and Mormon worship in three different chapels on the grounds. Leilani insisted that her little sister, Margaret, attend the Protestant, Kanaana Hou Church, but Margaret liked to stay in bed pretending not to hear her sister's entreaties. Finally, Leilani sent a faithful, if thin-witted patient named Lazaro, who drove a dilapidated truck under Margaret's window and tooted the horn until the rest of the girls threw her out, a Jonah-like sacrifice to the noisy Lazaro. Margaret liked the Hawaiian singing at the Kanaana Hou Church but she hated the "long, boring sermons" by the lay-minister Koni. Sunday afternoons, patients gathered from the three different churches and spent the remainder of the day at picnics, games or dances.

Week after week, Margaret's routine seldom varied and week after week, Wiley Kihe was there. He walked Margaret home from her job on the wharf. He escorted her to the movies and to the dances in Kalaupapa's social hall. He crowded in behind her in the hospital waiting line. He gave her gifts, including a necklace from Tomita's store. "It was only one cheap necklace," Margaret remembers, "but something you appreciate. You say, 'Oh, my boyfriend gave me this!' to your friends and they impress." It wasn't long until Margaret went with Wiley for long walks in the moonlight and joined him in the shady grove near Mother Marianne's grave.

Ignoring the protests of her sister, Leilani, her friend, Carrie, and her parents on Oahu, Margaret married Wiley Kihe in the small social hall of St. Francis Catholic Church. Ida sent a silver wedding band. Carrie and a few friends from Bishop made up the wedding party. Leilani and her new patient husband stood beside the bride and groom. Father Peter married the two teenage outcasts, and after celebrating over beer at Tomita's, the young couple moved Margaret out of Bishop into a one-room apartment.

Margaret remembers, "I was lonely. To me, Wiley was one very handsome man. Every day our friends were dying. Sometimes we bury two, three people in one day. How many times we walk by the sea down Kamehameha Street to the Catholic or to the Protestant cemeteries, say 'good-bye.' Not all old people, either. Young people. Many. Leprosy nevah have cure then, you know. We all going die. Why not get married? Why not try be happy? Short time we live."

But Margaret and Wiley's happiness was very short-lived. "After we get married," Margaret explained, "sometimes Wiley no work. Just go ovah Tomita's and drink and drink. Then he get my paychecks and spend 'em at the bar. Come home with nothing. If I late from work he yell at me and beat me with his belt and tell me I was seeing other man. I would cry and say 'I no see anyone' but it no matter to Wiley. He beat me again. I nevah know what to do. When I little my mother and father beat me. I think maybe God rescue me from that when I come Kalaupapa. Then I marry Wiley and he beat me too. I more and more lonely every day."

There was some good news just after Margaret's fifteenth birthday. On her Saturday checkup at the Kalaupapa Clinic the doctor discovered in the course of other tests that Margaret was pregnant. Because of Margaret's pregnancy, the administrators provided a small cottage for the young couple. Margaret was given a job in the hospital. She knew the baby would be taken from her. She knew her child would be sent to Oahu or even to the mainland to be adopted by another couple to prevent it from contracting her disease. She knew she probably would never see the baby again, but still she sewed baby clothing and worked on a fine baby quilt to wrap the baby in for its trip up over the *pali.*

Whereas Margaret felt good about the baby, the news of Margaret's pregnancy only depressed Wiley further. He spent more and more time away from her drinking at Tomita's store with his young friends. Late at night he would stumble drunk to their rooms and beat Margaret for no reason other than the ongoing frustration of his life on Molokai.

One night Wiley lay on their mattress too drunk to move. For a moment his young bride stared at her fresh crop of bruises and then back to her unconscious husband snoring loudly on the bed, the belt still in his hand. Quietly, Margaret tiptoed from the room and ran down the trail, across the Waihanau stream bed and up Pahua Street to Bishop Home. Carrie was just leaving for the Friday night dance.

"Margaret, you look bad." Carrie reached out to embrace the sobbing friend.

Back in her old room at Bishop Home, Margaret shared the misery of her marriage. Carrie listened. Margaret told how Wiley invited his friends home for a drink after working on the garbage truck all day to impress the young men with his pretty wife. His friends would tease Wiley saying, "You ugly man to have such a beauty." Wiley answered, "Yeah, but nobody can take her. She stay faithful to me." When his friends laughed and answered,

"She faithful like one daughter and you her ugly old father," Wiley forced Margaret to smoke and to drink in front of them to prove he hadn't robbed the cradle.

Carrie let Margaret pour out her grief and anger. Then she spoke. "Come to da dance with me. You need one night free from dat guy. Come on, we going escape like our night in Waikiki. You can dance *Kā'eke'eke* again. O.K., girl?"

Carrie and Margaret joined the others enroute to the Friday night dance at the social hall. They sat, talked with their friends, ate *pūpū* [Hawaiian snacks] and drank fruit punch floating with fresh pineapple and papaya slices. Margaret was beginning to feel better when one of Wiley's friends rushed up to her.

"Wiley stay down da beach," he whispered. "He like see you."

Carrie grinned coyly at Margaret. "Maybe he sorry, Margaret. Go talk."

Margaret followed the boy from the room past the BayView Home and down to the little beach below the construction camp.

"Where Wiley stay?" Margaret asked suspiciously as they walked farther and farther away from the Kalaupapa Settlement. "He was too drunk to walk dis far."

Silently the young man pulled her even farther into the darkness. No longer could she hear the music playing or the dancers' voices through the stillness. Suddenly the young man turned and took her in his arms.

"You too good for Wiley, Margaret. He beat you. I make you happy now."

Margaret remembers crying out with fear. "I cannot. He's my husband. Please let me go. I cannot!"

Margaret broke free, scrambled up the bank and ran back towards the social hall. The boy on the beach yelled after her,

"You too good for him, Margaret. Come with me. I make you happy."

Margaret didn't stop running until she reached the hall.

It was difficult to hide her terror from the other girls.
Trembling, she had barely seated herself beside them
when Wiley Kihe, still drunk and very angry, stumbled
into the room looking for his missing wife. When he
spotted her, he shouted,

"Why you leave me to come here dis dance?"

People stopped talking. Dancers watched silently as
Wiley strode across the room, grabbed Margaret by the
hair and yanked her back into the darkness. Carrie tried to
intervene but Wiley brushed her away with one arm and
with the other half dragged, half carried Margaret across
the settlement to their cottage.

When Margaret tried to explain, Wiley beat her. When
she denied any impropriety, he beat her again. When she
broke down and tearfully told what his friend had done,
Wiley picked up an old lamp pole and beat her with it.
Leaving his young wife half-conscious, Wiley stalked out
into the night in search of the man who had tried to steal
her from him.

Apparently, the beatings caused premature labor and
two days later Margaret was taken to the hospital in great
pain. Dr. Tuttle was on vacation. Dr. Hirschey, his wife,
and several nurses were on detail all night trying to aid a
whole hospital full of emergency cases, some related and
some unrelated to leprosy. In the bed next to Margaret
was a large Hawaiian woman heavy with the disease.
Margaret remembers that the woman began to gasp; the
tracheotomy tube through which she breathed had clogged
with mucous. Margaret, still in labor, tried to call the
doctor, but the entire staff was working with several
serious emergencies in a different room. With the suction
instruments unavailable, the large woman, choking to
death, grabbed up a pair of scissors from the table and
plunged it into her own throat, trying to relieve the
pressure. By the time the nurse arrived, the woman had
bled to death.

At approximately the same moment, Margaret gave

birth to her first child. When the nurse put the little infant boy in her arms and asked Margaret to name him, she smiled with delight.

"I call him Wiley, after husband," she said.

The nurse suddenly realized that Margaret misunderstood.

"I'm sorry, child," the nurse explained. "Your baby is dead. We only asked you for a name because it is necessary before the baby's burial."

Slowly, Margaret handed her dead baby back to the nurse. She watched her take little Wiley away to have him buried. Tears flooded down her cheeks.

"I cried a long time," she remembers. "I lie there thinking about my husband and that dirty licking he gave me with a lamp pole. He hit me right across the stomach. He kill my baby. When the baby come out had one 'black and blue' right across where Wiley beat me with the pole. The baby was ovah ten pounds. So sad to be born with no life inside. Doctor Hirschey say that baby dead for two days. Lying in the hospital I think it be good to be dead just like my baby. I remember the lady who cut her throat and died in the cubicle next to me. I think maybe she lucky to die."

The tall Hawaiian woman sat in a chair across from Margaret's hospital bed. She wore a neat white nurse's dress, with white shoes and a tiny red rose bud on her lapel. Margaret awakened and saw the woman sitting there, reading an Hawaiian Bible like her own. For a moment she thought it was Sarah Bunker come to visit on Kalaupapa.

"Hello, Margaret. You've been sleeping a long time."

Margaret stared uncomprehendingly at the woman. Suddenly she remembered her dead baby and began to cry. Her unknown guest didn't look embarrassed by her tears.

"It's good to cry," she said. "In fact, sometimes when terrible things like this happen, there's very little else we can do."

The woman stood and walked over to the bed. She took a clean, white handkerchief from her dress and handed it to Margaret.

"I'm sorry your baby died."

Margaret moved to turn away, but before she could roll over on her side, the woman moved closer.

"My name is Alice Kahokuoluna. I'm the new pastor at the Kanaana Hou Church."

"What happened Reverend Koni?" Margaret asked, surprised.

"He retired and I've come to replace him," she explained.

"I no go that church anymore," Margaret continued. "Koni boring. The people talk long words. I nevah understand nothing."

The Reverend Alice moved a chair closer to Margaret's bed and listened intently as the child poured out her anger and loneliness. Alice Kahokuoluna was the first Hawaiian woman ordained by the Congregational Churches of Hawaii. For sixteen years before arriving on Kalaupapa, she had served the historic Hana Church in Maui. When the pastor at Kalaupapa's leprosarium resigned, Reverend Alice volunteered to take his place. During her first weeks of ministry, she could not force herself to look at the deformed and suffering members of her congregation. She preached instead to the little window over the back door and hoped her people heard. Gradually, Reverend Alice built up the courage to look at her flock, and for eighteen years, she served them faithfully.

When Margaret finished her story, the Reverend Alice's eyes were wet with tears. She stared down at the little girl. For a moment, she didn't speak. She had no easy answers to pass like sugar pills among the dying.

"When my husband died," Alice finally began, "I cried

just like you. There were days I felt like crying all day long. So I walked in the garden when I cried and planted and trimmed and fertilized my roses. The roses got more water that year than ever before."

Margaret smiled.

"When you can't stop crying, Margaret, plant some roses. Then one day when you feel like laughing again, you'll have rosebuds to give away."

Then Reverend Alice bowed her head, closed her eyes, and began to pray the Lord's prayer in her native Hawaiian:

> *E ko makou Makua i loko o ka lani*
> [Our Father, who art in heaven . . .]

Slowly, Margaret joined in that prayer:

> *E kali mai hoi ia makou i ka makou*
> [Forgive us our sins as we forgive those who
> sin against us . . .]

When the prayer ended, Reverend Alice took the rosebud off her lapel and handed it to Margaret.

"The doctor says you'll be out of here soon. I want you to come visit me the day you leave the hospital. I have some roses we can plant together."

Then with a smile and a wave, the Reverend Alice continued on her hospital rounds.

Margaret approached the white picket fence around the parsonage across from the Kanaana Hou Church. The patients were not allowed in the buildings of any nonpatient residence. There was great fear even in 1938 that leprosy was far more contagious than it is. Margaret pulled the long cord that rang the bell over Reverend Alice's front door. Almost immediately, the door swung open and

Reverend Kahokuoluna bounded down the stairs and up
the little rock pathway to the gate.

"Margaret, you've come just in time! We're going for a
ride over to old Kalawao Town."

Seeing Margaret's puzzled look, she continued, "Don't
worry. We'll be back before lunch and no one will miss us."

Alice led Margaret to her old Dodge that had taken on
all the rusty welts of its leprous surroundings. The motor
coughed several times before the car lurched forward.

"My, my. I'll never get it right!" Alice groaned, as the
car threw them forward, then backward against the seat
several times. Finally, after gasping and wheezing down
the dirt driveway, the old car made its way up Damien
Road toward the Kalawao side.

"I've found the perfect place for you to plant your
roses," Alice shouted above the car's rattling din.

Still Margaret rode in silence, wondering if this *pupule*
[crazy] lady really did know where they were going. As
the road dipped down the crater's side, the entire bay
glistened in the morning sun. Suddenly, Alice stepped on
the brakes and the car slid to a dusty stop near a large
tangle of jungle. Alice jumped out of the car and started
down the path; Margaret struggled to keep up. There were
red and yellow hibiscus vines hanging in full bloom on the
kukui trees. Among the ground cover, hundreds of bright
orange *kīkānia* grew. A covy of wild *nēnē* [Hawaiian
geese] broke loudly from their hiding place and half flew,
half ran down the road toward Kalawao. Alice stopped
quickly. Margaret stumbled into her.

"Look!" Alice said, pointing as though to a chest of
buried treasure.

Margaret looked.

"At the church?" Margaret said, obviously disappointed.

"Yes," Alice said, her enthusiasm growing by the
second. "At the church. Look, isn't it beautiful?"

"It one church," Margaret said. "Same every other
church."

Alice waded through the tangle of long grass and lantana

and climbed up the stairs of the old wooden building, half-hidden by vines and ferns and *kukui* trees. Though swollen into its frame by tropical rain and hot, island sunshine, the door finally gave way to Alice's persistent pull. Slowly, she walked into the dirty, abandoned wood frame building with all the awe a peasant shows a great cathedral.

"This is not like every other church, Margaret. This is Siloama, the Church of the Healing Springs."

Margaret wasn't impressed, but she sensed the excitement radiating from this strange woman and began to feel that excitement herself. Alice walked up and down the aisle. She dusted off the dirt-covered dedication plaque with her hands and wiped off the dust on her clean, white dress. Finally, she stopped.

"There's nothing we can do today, Margaret, but imagine what we can do this Saturday with brooms and mops and buckets of hot, sudsy water!"

Margaret's embryonic enthusiasm for the place began to dwindle.

"We will make it shine as it used to shine when the patients built it long ago." Alice walked up and down the aisle. "The world knows about the heroic priests and nuns who came to serve the victims of leprosy on Molokai," said Alice Kahokuoluna enthusiastically, "and that is good. But few people know of the Protestant Christian patients who landed here almost a decade before Damien and built this first church.

"It's tragic that we know almost nothing about them," she added, "but we do know that in their moment of misery, they built this church. And we must help it live again. They planted roses, Margaret, even while they suffered; and we are going to dig around those roses and water and feed them until they bloom again!"

Leilani sat in an old, torn lawn chair in front of Margaret's cottage. She munched wild cherries pulled from a nearby tree. Margaret greeted her older sister and sat down in the grass beside her. Wiley was over at Tomita's, drinking with his friends. Neither of the two girls spoke.

Margaret and her sister had never been close friends, even when drawn together by their disease on the island of Molokai. The enmity between them reached far back. Their mother, Edith, favored Leilani and gave Margaret away to Moriah and William. Edith also reported Margaret's leprosy to the Board of Health when it looked as though Leilani might go to Molokai alone. On the island, Leilani acted the role of the stern, elder sister. She had opposed Margaret's marriage to Wiley and wrote often to both sets of parents, telling how Wiley beat and generally mistreated Margaret. Leilani's reports caused Margaret's father William to be so angry that he invoked an Hawaiian death curse on Wiley.

"When Wiley die," he promised, "he die of one great growing ball in his stomach."

The Hawaiian curse was not taken lightly by Wiley, so Leilani's reports only added to Margaret's misery. Still, when their Uncle George died shortly after Margaret's arrival on Molokai, Leilani was Margaret's only blood relative on the island. They visited each other occasionally, but conversation was strained. The two girls sat in silence, if for no other reason, because there was very little to talk about, given the aching tedium of the leprosarium routine. Finally, Leilani broke the silence.

"Dis probably da last cherry I going eat!"

Margaret looked up, startled.

"Why you say that?" she asked.

Leilani looked far down the island toward the sea.

"Last Saturday, when I wade for *'opihi*, one big wave knock me down. I almost drown. Today we go for *'opihi* again. But I no think I make chowder tonight."

Sensing her own impending death, Leilani had come to say good-bye. Awkwardly, she embraced her startled sister, then wandered off to Bishop Home. It was one of those moments that Margaret wishes she had a chance to live again. There was so much unsaid between them. But the opportunity for two estranged sisters to be reconciled was lost forever.

Later, Margaret learned that Leilani visited her good friend, Mrs. Luddington, on the staff of Bishop Home to tell her of those same ominous intuitions. Then, together with three other friends, Leilani drove across the island to Kalawao Town. They turned left, near the old Siloama church and drove along the cliffs looking for a good place to descend into the coral tide-pools to pry off the dark, coolie-hatted *'opihi* urchins. The small muscle that anchored the urchin's shell to the slippery rocks was delicious, much-prized by Hawaiian tastebuds.

The ocean was calm, the tide exceptionally low. The two women and two men waded into the tide-pools, filling their string-net bags with an abundant catch of urchins. Without fear, they walked right to the edge of the tide-pools, concentrating on the small black creatures, ignoring the movement of the sea. Finally, walking barefoot over a wide, flat rock, they turned their backs on the sea altogether. A wave broke over them and swept them backwards into the deep and treacherous waters beyond. The men tried to swim for shore. Leilani and her friend, Mary, couldn't swim.

A patient on the coral nearby ran to the beach for a rope. His friends held the end of the rope, and the patient plunged into the sea to rescue the girls. The waves were building in size as the tide came in; the girls were flung against the coral. The young patient struggled futilely against the sea.

Word of the rescue operation spread rapidly to the settlement. Doctor Tuttle and many of the patients raced to the site. Mary Morita was pulled to the shore first, but she died in the arms of her rescuer. By the time they pulled Leilani to the cliffs, her body was bloody, battered to death on the rocks even before the sea could drown her.

*   *   *

The long procession of mourners stretched the entire length of Kamehameha Road from Kalaupapa Town to the Papaloa Cemetery. Patients, themselves in various stages of death, walked in silence behind the mothers of the two drowned girls. Mary Morita's mother came down the *pali* [cliffs] on horseback to her daughter's wake. Leilani's mother, Edith, came by steamer to Kalaupapa's wharf. Charles Frederick was in such great shock over his eldest daughter's death that he remained at home in Honolulu and mourned there, alone.

Margaret thought she was immune to the quiet misery of these beachfront death parades. She had seen enough of them in her short tenure on Molokai. Two or three times a day, small clusters of friends and family followed the caskets of their loved ones en route to burial in the Catholic, the Protestant or the Mormon cemeteries along the sea. But as the crowd of mourners began to sing "Saviour, Like a Shepherd, Lead Us," Margaret thought of the tiny casket of her son that she had only recently followed up this same road. When she stood between Wiley and Leilani's husband, Johnny, on the edge of her sister's grave, she could see the still unmarked grave of her own child nearby. Furiously, she blinked back the tears as the great crowd prayed the Lord's prayer together.

Margaret looked up at the two young men, one on each side of her. Her husband Wiley stood there trembling from the long, sleepless night. Leilani's husband, Johnny, stood nearby in the same condition. Both men had been afraid to sleep in their cottages.

"Leilani's death not good," Margaret explained. "Hawaiian people believe the dead must finish what not finished in life." Both men had wronged Leilani in life and were afraid she would avenge her sorrow in death. They didn't want to be trapped with her ghost if that ghost should return in the "haunted hours" before the wake. So

Margaret consented to sleep alongside them on the beach below the Visitor's Quarters. She had been sound asleep when Wiley awakened, screaming.

"Look! Look! You sister standing dere in her brown velvet dress."

Margaret awakened, looked sleepily up and down the deserted beach and saw nothing.

"I no see nothing!" Margaret remembers answering. "I tired. Go sleep. Let me rest."

But all night, the two boys lay awake, haunted by their guilt. Wiley hated Leilani for her opposition to his marriage to Margaret. He hated her for reporting the beatings to Margaret's parents in Honolulu. So he teased and taunted and made life generally miserable for his sister-in-law. Johnny had his own reasons for feeling guilty. Margaret watched them praying the Lord's prayer together at Leilani's grave, but could not join with them in that prayer.

"I very young and very angry," Margaret remembers. "I saw too many people die already for be so young. I think God no care. How come so many suffer if God care? How come so many die? I look at all those faces around me praying. So ugly, those faces. So twisted and stumped and broken, those bodies. They hate and fight and fear each other. Still they pray. And still no answer. So I don't pray. Too many people die to keep on praying."

Margaret heard the honking outside her cottage window. Her husband, still drunk and exhausted from his Friday night at Tomita's, snored beside her in the bed. Margaret rolled over and tried to go back to sleep. Still the horn sounded. Finally, she groaned and rolled out of bed to see who was making all that racket. It was easy to guess. From her window, Margaret could see the Reverend Alice Kahokuoluna in her terminally-ill-but-still-able-to-crawl Dodge car. Rachael Kamaka sat beside her in the front seat. The back seat was crowded with girls from the Kanaana Hou Church.

"Good morning, Margaret," they said in a kind of practiced unison and then burst out laughing.

Margaret opened the door a crack and whispered loudly, "Oh, Mother Alice, I cannot go today. Too tired. Have to work later."

Alice came down from the car and walked to the little picket gate hanging half-off its hinges.

"Good morning, Makalika. I heard that today was your day off. A perfect day to plant roses, don't you think?"

Every Saturday since that first surprise visit to the jungle-covered church of Siloama Springs, the routine had been the same. Alice and Rachael packed a giant lunch, loaded mops and brooms, hammers and nails into the tired, old Dodge and rounded up the youth of Kanaana Hou Church for the ride across the Kalaupapa Peninsula to the Kalawao side for the rebuilding of Mother Alice's church.

Every Saturday, Margaret stood at the door and protested, but every Saturday Alice smiled and waited and talked of planting roses. Finally, this Saturday as always, Margaret threw on her clothing and, still protesting, joined the girls in the back seat of that car for their precarious journey alongside the crater to Kalawao Town.

Margaret didn't know why she always gave in to Mother Alice. She didn't know why she went back to the Kanaana Hou Church every Sunday, either. Certainly, the Reverend Kahokuoluna was an improvement over the last minister. In fact, Margaret had to admit she even enjoyed watching the dark, middle-aged Hawaiian lady in her long white dress walk across the platform of the church, open her old, Hawaiian Bible and tell them stories in Hawaiian and in English from its pages.

When Mother Alice preached, the people listened. They didn't shift their bodies restlessly like they used to or argue in loud whispers or gossip up and down the pews. Alice told them about other people who suffered, about

Naaman the *ma'i-Pākē* and his mudbath in the river, about David and his sin with Bathsheba and the death of his son, Absalom, with the long spear, about Zaccheus, the midget who sat in a tall *kukui* tree to see the Lord pass by, and about the luau-feast Jesus had in the tax collector's house.

Margaret even felt like praying again when Mother Alice bowed her head and talked to God in her quiet, loving way. Still, Margaret was always surprised when she left that warm cottage bed on her one day off from work at the hospital and climbed into the back seat of Alice's Dodge to spend the day in the dust and splinters of the Siloama Church.

Already, they had knocked down the jungle from its stranglehold on the little, wood building and its tower. They had cleaned the auditorium and repaired the broken pews and pulpit. They had weeded around the graves of those first members of the church and smoked a hive of bees from their home in the old church rafters.

"Today, girls, we clean the foundation!" Alice called over her shoulder at them as she bounded from the car and walked enthusiastically up the newly cut path through the long grass to the freshly painted porch of the old church.

"Foundation?" the girls called back. "Why clean da foundation?"

Alice led her protesting parade of girls carrying mops and brooms and shovels to the east end of the old church. She knelt down on the platform of rocks on which the building stood. The pulpit end of the church was completely overgrown with prickly *kīkānia* bushes. The lava stones were coated with decades of dirt, decayed leaves and thick spider webs.

"*Auwē!*" one of the girls groaned. "Why clean dat place? Nobody going see it anyway."

Alice only smiled, pulled on her gloves and began to swat at the bugs and spiders. Seeing that resistance, as usual, would be useless, the girls used their brooms to brush away the refuse convering the foundation and their shovels to clear a path around the foundation stones.

Floyd McHenry, one of Alice's regular helpers, joined the girls in their unpleasant task. He climbed down the foundation, hoping to find an old stone adze or poi pounder. Mother Alice followed. Together, they discovered a passageway from outside, under the pulpit end of the church. Alice called the girls to help remove the stones that had fallen over a short set of stairs. As they carried off the stones, they discovered a small, hidden vault.

"What dat?" a girl asked, pointing at the battered corner of a book sticking out of the vault.

Mother Alice reached down and pulled out a big ledger. The girls clustered around her as she opened the fragile, yellowed pages, covered in neat, Hawaiian script, and began to read. Soon great tears trickled down her cheeks as the full meaning of this carefully written record dawned upon her. This was the missing history of the Siloama Church. It had been stored there in 1927 when the first leprosarium on Molokai was moved from Kalawao Town to the warmer and less windy side of the Kalaupapa peninsula.

All morning, Mother Alice and her girls read the dusty pages in this book of revelation, records reaching back to that first forlorn landing of Hawaiian leprosy victims beneath the towering cliffs of Molokai. In that first crowd of outcasts, there were twelve women and twenty-three men from six Congregational churches on Oahu, one on Molokai, four on Maui, and four on the big island, Hawaii. In the days soon after their arrival, these brothers and sisters in Christ found each other. Together, they climbed up the hill and looked down on the pathetic beach where they had been abandoned and the handmade, palm-frond shelters or the wet caves beneath the *pali* where they were forced to live. Under a tree on this very spot, the Christian patients met. They were Christ's body, the church, gathered to pray, to sing hymns, to read their precious Hawaiian Bible, and to dream about the church building they would plant one day upon that place.

The meticulous Hawaiian notes in the large, business ledger were the work of J. H. Hao, a Christian leprosy patient elected treasurer of that first church among the patients on Molokai. His records explain why they named the church Siloam, after that pool in Jerusalem into which the ancient sufferer dipped to find comfort and healing when the angel of mercy stirred the waters. They would be Christ's pool of comfort to the miserable and to the dying. They would bring hope and healing to their fellow victims in that awful place.

In the ledger that Mother Alice read, those first years on Molokai were described as *"Aole Kanawai ma keia wahi* [No law in the place]. Without police or tribunal chaos often reigned. After five years, by 1873, there were 700 patients, mainly male leprosy victims in the last, horrible stages of the disease. These patients were especially hateful toward the white man who had insisted that victims of leprosy be separated from their friends and family when, in fact, the Hawaiians had no special fear of this disease.

Therefore, when Father Damien, a white *haole* [foreigner], arrived in 1873 to help minister to the patients, many of the patients, including Catholics, shunned him. In the old ledger, Mother Alice was thrilled to discover that the Protestant Christians on Kalaupapa realized how much this priest's presence could mean to the almost lawless colony and its dying inhabitants. They went up and down Kalawao encouraging the other patients to welcome Father Damien, assuring them he had come to bring life, not more death to this place. The world knew of Father Damien's eventual contribution to the victims on Molokai, but did not know that God used a courageous group of Protestant Christians to help Damien begin his ministry there.

The sun disappeared behind the crater before Mother Alice and her girls loaded into the old Dodge and headed back towards Kalaupapa Town. Beside the two women on the front seat, rode the precious book. That little band of Protestant Christians sixty-five years before—in their own day of misery—had stopped to plant a rose bush, and it had bloomed again for Mother Alice and her girls. Suddenly, the driver of that rickety, old car began to sing above the rattles.

> *Hoonani i ka Makua mau,*
> *Ke Keiki me ka Uhane no.*
> *Ke Akua mau-hoomaikai pu*
> *Ko Keia ao, ko kela ao.*

"Praise God from whom all blessings flow," Mother Alice sang, and one by one, Margaret and her friends joined in the singing.

Margaret was pregnant with her second child. Symptoms of her leprosy worsened with each day of pregnancy. Although the doctors continued their applications of carbon dioxide snow and chaulmoogra oil, Margaret's condition did not improve. Her body began to swell. Red sores formed on her legs and torso. She couldn't walk. She lay on her cottage mattress with a high fever, her body shaking with chills. The little hospital overflowed with emergency patients. There was no room for Margaret. Though a nurse, Mary Ann Fuller, visited with pills to ease her discomfort, Margaret grew thin. Her urine darkened. She thought she would die, or worse, that again, her baby would be born dead.

Wiley was disgusted by the changes in his pretty, young wife. No longer could he invite his friends to their cottage to have a drink and admire her. So he spent his days working on the garbage detail and his nights drinking and flirting with other women. Wiley left Margaret alone. Often she had to crawl from bed and across the cottage floor to make a meal. On those occasions when friends would visit, they were too embarrassed to talk about her husband's antics.

When she felt again the pains of labor, fellow patients rushed her to the hospital. All through the night she waited and, as the sun rose over Kauhako crater, Margaret gave birth to her second child, a tiny baby girl. She named the baby Mary Ann, after the kindly nurse who had helped her through her illness and pregnancy.

At 8:00 A.M., Nurse Mary Ann Fuller walked into the tiny hospital cubicle with her namesake in her arms. Margaret looked up at the child wrapped in the baby blanket she had made for her son and saved for her second-born.

"She is a beautiful child, Margaret."

The nurse looked down at the baby and then up to the baby's young mother.

"I can hold her?" Margaret asked.

"No," the nurse said sadly. "It is time we take her up the *pali* [mountain]."

"So young to make such a journey," answered Margaret. "Who going carry her?"

"I will," answered Mary Ann Fuller. "You've named her after me," the nurse said proudly, "and no one else is careful enough to carry her up the mountain."

Margaret smiled. "*Aloha 'oe* [may you be loved]," she said to her baby. "*Māhalo* [thank you]," she said to Mary Ann.

Quickly, the nurse turned and walked from the room. Margaret stared out the window, hoping she would see her beautiful, newborn daughter one more time. She lay there picturing the nurse mounting the horse and then riding the long, steep trail up the mountainside. She pictured her little Mary Ann in the nurse's arms and determined that one day she would see her child again.

Margaret and Wiley had three other children on Molokai, all boys: Edwin, Elsworth and Charles. The law required that each child be taken from his mother and offered for adoption. Four times, Margaret watched her children carried up the *pali*, and four times, she vowed to beat leprosy and be reunited with her children. Wiley Kihe was not so fortunate.

On their tenth wedding anniversary, Wiley, aged twenty-eight, still showed few signs of leprosy. His hands and his mouth were only slightly affected. Then, suddenly, Wiley grew very ill. Something was growing in his stomach. His bowels no longer moved on their own. He lay in terrible pain. He could not forget Margaret's father's curse: "You going die from one large ball in you stomach." The doctors diagnosed the ball as terminal cancer in its final stages.

The priest stood just outside their bedroom and quietly closed the door.

"He is dying, Margaret."

Margaret nodded, but felt nothing.

"I have heard his confession," the priest continued, "but he needs you to forgive him."

Margaret put down her dishtowel and walked into their bedroom. Wiley lay on his back, his face twisted in pain. The sheet was wet with sweat.

"Margaret," Wiley gasped up at her. "Please forgive me for all da dirty things I did to you. How mean . . . and I scarred you up and everything. Please forgive."

Margaret remembers looking down at her young husband. The priest moved in beside her and whispered,

"Please forgive him. If you do, he will die in peace."

Margaret remembered the good times, the shell necklace from Tomita's store that Wiley bought her, the picnics at Kalawao, and the long walks in the moonlight when they were first in love.

"I forgive," she said simply and sat down beside him. "I forgive, Wiley."

He reached for her hand, but before he touched her, Wiley died.

"I so glad I forgive, Wiley," remembers Margaret. "What if he die and I no forgive? What if I live all my life with that anger inside me? Bad! Best to forgive right away."

Dr. Norman Sloan, the medical director of the Kalaupapa Settlement Hospital, looked intently at a patient's foot, then up to Margaret standing nearby.

"Good job, Margaret," he said to her. "You should be the doctor and I should be the nurse's aide."

Margaret grinned at the doctor's compliment, but said nothing. In the year since Wiley's death, Dr. Sloan had trained her well. Before he made his hospital rounds, Margaret visited a patient with her wagon and instrument tray. Carefully, she cut away the old bandages, tossed them in the disposal unit on the wagon. Then she swabbed the open sore with peroxide to clean and disinfect it, covered the clean sore with sterilized gauze and called the doctor to begin his inspection or operation to remove gangrenous bones or clean away dead or infected tissue.

Often on her rounds, she had a volunteer to push the cart. Obert Nahoikaika was, as Margaret remembers him, "a plain Hawaiian boy, pure Hawaiian. Chubby, but not so bad. Tall, but only tall by me and very nice." Obert fell in love with Margaret that first day she ordered him out of his hospital bed, cut off his bandages, dressed his sores, called for the doctor, made sure the doctor dressed the wound correctly—and all without saying "good morning" or "please." After his infected foot had healed, he volunteered to help Margaret on her rounds and followed her about the hospital each day muttering, "Look at dat girl. Isn't she *he mea 'e* [a wonder]!"

One of Obert's weaknesses was volleyball. That fairly short and chubby Hawaiian with crippled, leprous hands, could really fool the opposition with a sudden burst of speed or an unexpected jump shot, slammed down across the net. He was a reliable and skilled member of the team. Then he met Margaret. At 5:00 P.M. sharp, no matter what was happening on the volleyball court, Obert left the game. He ignored his friend's loud complaints, rushed to the hospital, picked up his favorite nurse's aide, and delivered her safely home.

Beer was Obert's other vice. Almost everyone in Kalaupapa drank it. Bull Dog Ale was the leprosy patient's best friend. It anesthetized the pain and the loneliness of the island's isolation. Tourists sailing by that picturesque peninsula or riding down the *pali* on a mule tour of the leprosarium saw the beauty of that place, but for the patients who lived a lifetime there, it was little better than imprisonment. And they were ill besides, and bored and tired of the routine that led them nowhere. Their children were shipped away at birth. The government owned their houses and their land. The hopelessness of their disease moved them inexorably towards helplessness. So bottles and bottles of Bull Dog Ale flowed down throats, dulled senses, loosened tongues and somehow helped to make life more bearable.

Obert's sudden addiction to Margaret caused his team to lose the Settlement's championship and his long-term addiction to Bull Dog Ale gave him cirrhosis of the liver. Thirty days after Obert met Margaret in the hospital, he returned there, terminally ill. Leprosy doesn't usually kill its victims. The disease destroys resistance and the patient usually falls prey to various other complications his body can no longer resist.

Margaret stood at the end of Obert's hospital bed. "What? You back here again?" she scolded him.

"Only fo'a see you, Margaret," Obert answered. "Will you marry me?"

Margaret laughed and shook his bed-frame playfully. Dr. Sloan called from across the room. In the hallway, he told Margaret that Obert's blood tests were conclusive. He would die within the next few months. There was nothing the doctors could do to prevent liver failure.

Margaret walked back to Obert's bed.

"So you really sick dis time, eh? Well, Margaret take care you. You going play volleyball again. No worry." Obert took her hand. "Margaret, will you marry me?" he asked again, this time obviously serious.

"Not today, Obert," she teased gently. "Maybe tomorrow, after breakfast. Now go sleep. You liver need rest. You work 'em too hard with all that Bull Dog Ale."

Margaret walked quickly from the room. Dr. Sloan was still in the hallway, talking to a nurse. When he finished, Margaret told him her news.

"Obert wants me to marry him. And I think I will."

Dr. Sloan was shocked. "He's going to die, Margaret. You can't marry him. He'll never leave the hospital again."

Margaret looked up at the doctor. "O.K., I marry him," she said, and walked away, leaving Dr. Sloan shaking his head with surprise.

Obert left the hospital for their wedding, but returned the next day. Within the month, he died.

"I feel sorry for him," Margaret explained. "He love me and he need me. What else?"

Visitors came rarely in the early days at Kalaupapa. People were afraid to expose themselves to a disease thought so contagious. The patients were embarrassed and shamed by their physical deformities. It was an expensive journey to sail to Molokai. The horseback ride down the steep and dangerous trail to the settlement was difficult. The patients' families were usually poor, trapped by demanding work schedules or unemployment.

However, as it became more and more apparent that leprosy was not as contagious as once believed, and with the added convenience of the little landing strip built at Kalaupapa, more and more visitors did arrive. Lawrence M. Judd, former governor of the Hawaiian Territory, was appointed chief administrator of Kalaupapa. He arranged that some of his celebrity acquaintances visit the island peninsula to encourage the patients. A visit by a famous athlete or a movie star was an important occasion to break up the patients' dull routine.

Margaret still remembers with delight two of those celebrity appearances. Shirley Temple came to visit a patient in Margaret's ward. "She no scared, you know," recalls Margaret of the visit by the famous actress. "She had one basket of roses and gave one rose to every patient. And, oh, to us was one holiday to have such a famous person visit here. Was good." Not to be outdone by the famous lady, two equally famous gentlemen soon paid a call on the patients at Molokai.

Hundreds of patients stood along the runway in the hot afternoon sun. Mr. and Mrs. Judd and other administrators joined the medical staff in the little cement-block building that served as control tower and waiting room for the Kalaupapa Airport. Other patients lined Kamehameha Street, down which the procession would pass bearing the awaited film stars. Delayed by a late take-off from Honolulu, the plane was overdue and hundreds of pairs of eyes squinted against the sun to see the small, four-seat aircraft make it is approach and landing.

As the plane touched down and taxied toward the welcome committee, hundreds of leprosy patients surged enthusiastically across the rope barrier and almost en-

gulfed the plane. Their disease-scarred faces stared up at
the little windows, searching for their famous guests.
Their crippled hands were extended and applauding. At
last, the door was opened and John Wayne, America's
original man of macho, the strong, silent champion of little
people, the fighter who used his fists and guns against
incredible odds at Iwo Jima and in the wild, wild West,
stepped out to greet them.

"He took one look at all us lepers staring at him,"
grinned Margaret, "then turn right around, got back into
the plane and closed the door. He said he not coming out,
seeing the patients, eh? Was scared. So he went back in."

The patients were confused and disappointed. Governor
Judd and his wife were stunned. The entire crowd waited
in silence. Nobody moved. No one knew what to do next.
But something happened inside the plane during those
next embarrassing minutes. Suddenly, the door opened
again. John Wayne and James Arness (of "Gunsmoke"
fame) stepped down into the crowd. The guests rode in
procession to the social hall where so many scratchy John
Wayne films had been seen and loved.

Mr. Wayne moved to the microphone. Again, the patients cheered, and finally, that tall gangly actor—already
a legend in his time—explained what happened on the
airfield that day.

"I came to give you courage," he said, "but I took one
look at what the disease has done to you and I knew I
couldn't do it. I wanted to go right back home. I was
scared, but my buddy here, James Arness, talked to me
and helped me get my wobbly legs out the door and down
the ramp. I'm sorry I was scared and I wish you well."

The patients cheered.

"We couldn't blame him, you know," said Margaret. "We
were all scared first time Kalaupapa. It takes some kin'
courage just to admit it."

Margaret was late for work at the hospital. She hurried
out the back door of her cottage, across the dirt yard and

untwisted the wire holding the chicken-coop door in place.

"Come here, dumb *moa!*" she shouted at the chickens. "I got you breakfast. *Moa! Moa!*" she clucked at them, tossing grain about the dirty, cement floor.

Two large chickens began to fight.

"No! No! Come here. No fight." Margaret swooped down and walked into the coop to separate the hens and spread the seed. After Margaret hosed new water into their trough and stirred up the gravel-feeder, she tossed a fallen piece of firewood onto the pile and hurried back into her kitchen for a quick cup of coffee before bolting down Haleakala Street and across the Bishop Home grounds to the hospital.

"Click. Click." At first, Margaret hardly noticed the quiet tapping sound that seemed to follow her about the room. "Click. Click. Click." She stopped to listen. The sound stopped. "Click. Click. Click." It began again when she continued walking across the kitchen floor.

Margaret stopped. What was making that sound? Every time she walked, she heard the clicking. Like taps on dance shoes, she thought. But she wasn't wearing shoes. She sat down and crossed her legs to inspect each foot. Sticking to her left sole was a wooden shingle held there by a long, rusty nail. Leprosy had killed the feelings in both feet long ago. She pulled out the nail and went to work.

All day long, Margaret rushed through the hospital corridor, pushing her cart with its tray of instruments and its rolls of gauze and bandages. Towards the end of the day, she bounced up the little step that separated the old hospital from its new, wooden wing, and without slowing down, banked the corner sharply, narrowly missing Dr. Sloan.

"Margaret, slow down," he told her. "Or you are going to run over somebody."

"No time, Doctor Sloan," Margaret answered. "Too many patients. Not enough help."

She continued on her rounds without looking back, but Dr. Sloan called out to her.

"Hold it, Margaret," he ordered, walking up to her. "What's that on your shoe?"

Margaret looked down. Her left shoe oozed with blood. Dr. Sloan helped Margaret to a chair, untied her shoe and examined the wound made earlier that day by the rusty nail.

"Margaret, this foot is in terrible shape. And this one, too," he said, looking at her right sole as well. "You will check into surgery right now and we'll see how bad the damage is."

Margaret complained, "I no feel nothing. Why cut?"

How many times Dr. Sloan had explained to his patients that, though leprosy had destroyed their valuable pain sensors, infection could still develop in their cuts and burns and punctures. Hands and feet should be constantly inspected for problem signs, he instructed; but few listened.

"Both feet have serious infections, Margaret," Dr. Sloan advised her. "We will have to amputate all your toes and the fronts of both your feet as well."

Margaret didn't return to her cottage for several weeks. It took months for her feet to heal. When they were healed, she cut off the sides of her shoes, strapped them to her feet, and began to teach herself to walk again.

The Kanaana Hou Church in Kalaupapa was crammed with patients right up to the dividing line. And in their area, the staff overflowed back out the doors and even leaned in the windows. The deacon rang the bell and Mother Alice walked down the aisle for the last time as their pastor. After the hymn had ended, after the Scripture was read and the prayers prayed, Mother Alice walked across the platform with her Hawaiian Bible in her arms, placed it on the pulpit, gripped the pulpit so tightly that her fingers turned white and began to pray.

"Oh, God, my work is complete here. Thy servant retires from active duty."

Margaret, sitting in the third row, bowed and wept with the other members of that congregation. For eighteen years, she had been Margaret's pastor, and Margaret's mind was as crammed with memories as those pews were crammed with believers because of Mother Alice's ministry among them.

"Whenever you need her," Margaret recalled, "you go her house and ring the bell and she put on the light and come. No matter what hour you go, she there. She good. Visit the sick. Visit the blind. In the hospital, she would stay by the bed when the patient dying. Praying, you know. And saying things to help like the 23rd Psalm. When the patient die, Mother Alice cry a little and finally she go home. She used to work on the choir. Practice. Practice. But one by one, every member in the choir die. Then she have to start again."

Mother Alice began her last sermon. "Eighteen years ago I didn't want to come to Molokai," she said to the crowd of worshipers. "I was afraid. At first, I couldn't even look at you and all your suffering. Then, one by one, I saw past the part of you that frightened me and I loved what I discovered there. You have taught me so much. I am grateful. What has been built here, we have built together."

Margaret remembered well at least one of those things they built together. "Every Saturday, we drove to Kalawao side to fix up dat Siloama Springs Church. Stay beautiful now. I went cook the stew or the pastry for lunch. Mother Alice pick us up in her car. We so happy, helping build our church. She wear overalls and work with Rachael Kamaka and Ethel Damon. Work hard. Was nice, you know."

"When I came here to be the pastor," Mother Alice concluded, "the patients were just waiting to die. Now, thanks to sulfone drugs—a gift from God—Hansen's disease is no longer the killer it once was. Today," she said, "Kalaupapa is not the land of the dead, but the land of the living. Thank God!"

When her sermon ended, Margaret said, "She raise her hand and bless us with God's blessing. Then she turn and wave good-bye. Mother Alice was sixty-nine when she left Kalaupapa. Later we learned she was dying of cancer. She always help us but nevah tell us that she sick, too. That lady planted a lot of roses on this place."

Margaret's condition continued to worsen. As if the increasingly crippled hands and the amputated feet were not enough, the leprosy continued to grow in her nose. One night, she awakened, struggling just to breathe. This time, her nasal passages and her larynx were bloated by billions and billions of leprosy bacilli. She was admitted to the hospital, already blue from lack of oxygen. Dr. Tuttle argued to postpone the tracheotomy. Dr. Sloan knew the risk, but Margaret's condition was too serious to delay. She lay there gasping as the two doctors debated.

Leprosy only grows actively in areas that are below normal body temperature. So, the deep, vital organs of the body—for example, the heart and lungs—are not affected. But wherever the body cools, in areas like the ears and the nose, the bacilli flourish.

Margaret remembers first getting a stuffy nose from the accumulating leprosy bacteria. Doctors tried to clear her nose by burning out the germs with silver nitrate. The stuffy nose condition worsened, so Margaret breathed through her mouth. As the flow of air cooled her throat, leprosy bacilli swarmed into the area. Lesions formed in the palate and the larynx. The walls of the larynx began to swell and the opening grew too small for breathing. Thus Margaret ended up in the emergency room, unable to breathe through either nose or throat.

The decision made, Dr. Sloan didn't even wait to anesthetize. He cut through her throat, made an opening below the larynx, and placed in that opening a tube through which Margaret could breathe. Margaret remembers, "Before, I used to kill my own chickens on Kalaupapa to cook. Then Dr. Sloan slit my throat. Was painful, you know. Nothing to numb it. They just plunge it into my throat. After that, I felt bad for the chickens. I know how they feel when we kill them. So I stop eating them, poor things."

"I write my mother, Ida. Tell her in five years after tracheotomy I going die. She come quick to Kalaupapa. She say, 'Baby, I tell you one last time: God give you life. Him the one take it away.' Then she noticed the handkerchief around my throat. She look aroun' see plenty patients with handkerchiefs. She say, 'Oh, baby, you get plenty cowgirls and cowboys here.' I say, 'What?' She say, 'Look there. What kind that they wear aroun' neck?' I laugh. I take off my neckerchief and show her the pipe sticking out of my throat. She cry. Say, 'I no like see.' But I show her anyway. She say, 'Where that pipe go?' I say, 'Down my throat so I can breathe.' She almost fainting. I tell her, 'Every day after I eat, I take the pipe out and clean it. But if I not put it back right away, the *puka* [hole] closes. I have to put vaseline and go slow, slow back into my throat until it goes down.' She stay in shock. Went home. Tell my father, William. He so upset. No wondah. That tube in my throat eight years, you know, before I breathe right again."

Joe King stood motionless at the bottom of a long, narrow canyon. He held a twenty-two rifle in readiness. Above and to the right, five other patients from Kalaupapa crept silently towards the edge of the ravine. Suddenly, one cried out and all five rushed in simultaneously, yelling and laughing and beating at the bushes with their hands. A large, wild pig, frightened by the commotion, charged down the ravine towards Joe King. He fired three shots into the giant animal before it dropped dead at his feet. The men cheered, loaded it on the truck they had borrowed from the Settlement, and raced down the mountain road toward Kalaupapa Town.

"We going have one big luau tomorrow, eh?" Danny Lee said, trying to get a can of Bull Dog Ale to his lips as the truck bumped wildly over the twisting, canyon road.

"You bet," answered Joe King. "One fine *pua'a* [pig] dat."

They had hunted until sunset and had almost given up hope of killing a pig for the feast. Now they hurried home, drinking, shouting congratulations to each other above the truck's noisy engine, anticipating that succulent treasure roasted twenty-four hours beneath the smoldering wood and hot luau stones.

Suddenly, a small deer ran across the road. Joe King swung the truck to miss it. The rear tire dropped off the roadway. The engines whined, trying unsuccessfully to pull the vehicle back onto the road-bed. The truck rolled once and settled heavily into the drainage ditch that fed the Waihanau stream bed. One by one, the men crawled out from under the wreckage. All but Joe King escaped the accident without a scratch. Joe lay beneath the truck, his ribs and right shoulder broken.

Joe remained in the hospital for weeks with a mangled collar bone, many broken ribs and a punctured lung. Everyday, Margaret passed his bed and everyday, she teased or scolded or encouraged him in his fight for recovery.

"Joe so sick, you know," Margaret recalls. "His leprosy bad so he not heal fast. Too weak to feed himself. So after work, I come sit by his bed and feed him."

In spite of all the care she showed him and all the expertise of Dr. Sloan and his medical staff, Joe's condition worsened. Finally, it was discovered that he had contracted tuberculosis. All the time they treated Joe's new illness, Margaret was there, helping on and off duty to make the man comfortable throughout his ordeal. Things went from bad to worse. An infection in his feet that a healthy person might easily have overcome became gangrenous. Doctors had to amputate both feet and one leg up to the kneecap. Still Margaret teased and scolded and encouraged Joe King to get well.

Soon after that unexpected day when the hospital finally released him, Joe and Margaret were married. His wooden leg was still on order from the mainland, so Margaret helped her new husband across the threshold of their tiny bungalow on Baldwin Street.

"We had one fine little house, Joe King and me," Margaret remembers. "It was up on the hill just above the meat house and the plumbing shop. Wonderful! We could see the ocean, just a bit, but could see. That house all wood with one tin roof. When the inspectors come, they always say, 'Margaret, your house look so old, but pretty and the inside so clean.' Joe work hard on the yard, even with his wood leg. He use the hand mower and trim everything. Him and I work together. I plant Hawaiian gardenias, the small, little one. We call them *kiele*. And I always plant roses, American Beauty. Something to give the other lepers when they sad. Nice to have something to give when people sad, you know.

"Joe was one good man. On my birthday, he buy me earrings. He know I love earrings. And he buy me new muumuu. Then wrap it. Take it home. Surprise me. And he save his money. Joe no drink up the money like others. He save it in one envelope. One birthday, he give me $100 he save.

"He was kind of jealous of me, though. At the hospital when I clean up the boys or dress their sores they say, 'Thank you, Margaret. Thank you, pin-up.' Then when they see me and Joe on the street, they say, 'Thank you, pin-up. I all right now.' And Joe would holler at them, 'Remember, that's my wife.' And I would tell him, 'Oh, Joe, that's just saying thanks.' But he would tell them, 'No touch. She mine.' I laugh, but I like that, you know.

"On Christmas, we had this big, black coral tree. I

decorate with red lights. And I had one white tree, too. We spray shaving cream on the real tree, put a little dip on each branch, and as the air get to it, it expand, expand, until it come all white and pretty. And I gather *kukū* in yard, that weed that stick to your pants. I spray it and make ornaments for the tree. And I had twenty-five cats. I love cats. And I had one nice table. And my cat, Pinti, was one big Persian cat. He like sit in his chair at that table. Nobody else sit there. No other cat either. And I had one tree for the cats with one bone for everyone of them. And when my neighbor come, he say, 'You know, I nevah see no cats get their own tree. But these cats have tree and they all underneath their tree, so proud, with all their bones.'

"We live sixteen years in that house. Good years. Joe was good. He work so hard, even with wood leg. Everyday he walk up Kamehameha to the cemetery and cut the grass or rake the dead stuff or shovel sand that came in with the storm that try to bury the graves. He was proud. It look good. When sulfone drugs come, people no die so much. Leprosy arrested by the new treatments. Not many buried anymore. Not like before. Two or three a day buried then. Cemetery was busy. Joe stay alone with the graves most of the time after sulfone. People get well. Go back home, leave Kalaupapa.

"But sulfone too late for me, for Joe, and for our friends. We the last of the lepers on Molokai. We live our whole life on that place. Sulfone come too late. Joe get sick with kidney. I try so hard to get him well. Everybody try. He not old, you know, only fifty. But his kidneys stop. I was very sad the day Joe died. I cannot stop crying. So I work on the roses like Mother Alice say. Then they bury Joe in his cemetery. I wondah if they will keep it nice like he keep it? I hope so. When Joe die, I know it is time for me to leave Molokai and go home again."

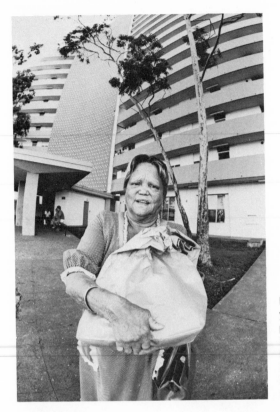

Left: After more than thirty years on Molokai as a leprosy patient, Margaret returned to Honolulu where she lives in a high-rise apartment building.
Below: Margaret in her one-bedroom apartment.
(Photos by Mark Kimura.)

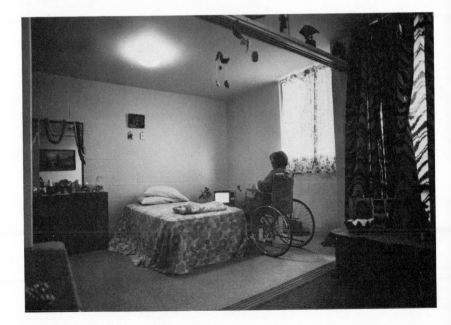

Left: Jackie Wiggins is the social worker who took Margaret to the Kalihi Union Church. She is one of many women who have made a significant difference in Margaret's life.
Below: The Rev. Jay Jarman, the former pastor of the Kalihi Union Church, was introduced to Margaret by Jackie Wiggins. (Photos by Mark Kimura.)

Above: Margaret and her "gang" of friends and fellow-workers at the Oahu Towers Project. **Below:** Margaret and her friend John Okada. When she found him, John was surrounded by cockroaches and filth waiting to die, but now he is an usher in the Kalihi Union Church and co-worker with Margaret in the Oahu Towers Project. (Photos by Mark Kimura.)

Above: It is an old Hawaiian custom to leave your shoes at the door upon entering a house or apartment. At this meeting of her "gang" Margaret's shoes are unique among those of her friends. **Below:** In Margaret's scrapbook is a picture of Shirley Temple taken when the movie star visited patients on Molokai. (Photos by Mark Kimura.)

Right: Margaret in her kitchen where she creates delicious cakes and cookies.
Below: Margaret still reads the Hawaiian Bible given her by Deaconess Sarah Bunker the day Margaret was taken to the Kalihi Hospital and diagnosed with leprosy.
(Photos by Mark Kimura.)

Above: Margaret at six and at fifty-nine, still dancing. (Photo at right by Mark Kimura.)

Margaret walks by the Kalihi Union Church in Honolulu. (Photo by Mark Kimura.)

Above: Margaret with her former pastor Jay Jarman (right) and author Mel White. **Below:** Mel White spent six months interviewing Margaret, visiting the leprosarium on Molokai, and researching leprosy with doctors and researchers. (Photos by Mark Kimura.)

"When you can't stop crying, plant some roses. Then one day when you feel like laughing again, you'll have rosebuds to give away." (Photo by Mark Kimura.)

IV.

OAHU
TOWERS
PROJECT

1969–

Margaret struggled up against her seatbelt to stare out the window of the little Air Polynesian six-seat Cessna as it circled the Honolulu International Airport. Below her passed the Aloha Tower from which she had sailed to Molokai a lifetime ago. The plane flew low over Kalihi and banked left over the freshly bulldozed fields that once held the Kalihi Receiving Station. Twelve-year-old Margaret had been delivered there by Mr. Kikila, the inspector from the Board of Health, before she was sent to Kalaupapa Leprosarium. The plane touched down and taxied to the Domestic Arrival terminal. Margaret had left Honolulu a beautiful young child. She returned bent and crippled and gray. No one was there to meet her.

Brown-skinned girls in yellow sarongs and muscular young men in tapa loincloths were draping tourist arrivals in colorful plumeria leis. Margaret inched her way through the crowd carrying one small suitcase and an orange *kīkānia* lei she had made for her father, William. He was ill. Her stepmother Ida was dead. Margaret was coming home for the funeral. She stood on the busy curb waiting for a bus ride into Honolulu.

A wealthy Chinese lady standing beside a large pile of luggage nearby looked at Margaret and began to speak rapidly to her son in Cantonese.

"Hey!" Margaret interrupted them. "I know you talking about me. No talk about me! What I did to you?"

The woman's embarrassed son stopped loading his mother's luggage into the Mercedes trunk and approached Margaret respectfully to explain his mother's mistake.

"My mother thought you look like a leper. But . . ."

Margaret cut him off. "Yes. So what."

The young man stared for a moment at Margaret's hands and feet, then, speaking rapidly to his mother, helped her into the back seat and locked the door. Hurriedly loading one last piece of luggage the young man said, "How come they let lepers come back from Molokai? You should stay there where you belong."

"I belong here," answered Margaret. "I was born here. And now I get one paper that say I can come here any time I like."

From inside the car the woman scolded her son in English. "Hurry! Hurry! Let's go."

"I stay well now—arrested!" Margaret hollered after them as the Mercedes squealed into the busy airport traffic. "I get paper for show proof."

Margaret remembers well that long process of being certified "an arrested leper." Test after test proved negative. The disease had left its trail of destruction on her body but the disease was dead. Margaret had won the battle. She boarded the downtown bus still trembling from her welcome home. "I angry. I no going let that happen to me, you know. People look. People whisper. No. I well now. Nobody stare at Margaret. If they don't accept me because I one leper I tell them, 'That your problem. Run away if you like. But I here and I going stay here.'"

After a long taxi ride up King Street, Margaret stood on the sidewalk in front of the Miyako Family Mortuary, her suitcase still in hand. A greeter at the funeral home took one look at this scarred mourner hobbling up the sidewalk, closed the funeral home doors and stood impassively in front of them.

"I'm sorry. You cannot enter here," he said, barring the doors.

Margaret thought about the Chinese woman and her son, the passengers who stared and whispered on that bus ride from the airport, the taxi driver who sped through the Honolulu streets to dump his deformed rider as quickly as he could. She met them all in those few short minutes after arriving in Honolulu. Now this ignorant young mortician blocked her way again.

"Thank you," Margaret said as she turned and walked away. She felt sad that she wouldn't see Ida's funeral and angry that they kept her out because of a disease that had already been arrested. But, the fight was gone. If they didn't want her in Honolulu, she would return to Kalaupapa. That was her real home anyway.

Margaret had one other stop to make before returning to Kalaupapa. She found her father William's little rented bungalow in Moiliili. She grasped the spindly railing and pulled herself up the splintered front steps. Through the torn screen she could see her father lying on a front room chair.

"William?" Margaret said, "It Margaret."

"Margaret, baby," he said, *"komo mai* [come inside]."

William was slowly and painfully dying from cancer of the mesentery. But when Margaret finished telling the story of her arrival in Honolulu and the reception at Miyako's, he stood, put on his coat and headed for the door.

"We going to sue them, baby. Not right what they doing." He leaned against a chair and began to weep. "First they take you away when you just my baby. Now when you old they like trow you out again."

Margaret moved to her dying father's side.

"It O.K., Papa. You rest now. Margaret going help you come strong again. We show them."

For six months Margaret seldom moved away from her father's side except for an occasional breath of air on the front porch or a quick hobble down to the all-night market on University Avenue. This routine was only interrupted for one week when she was admitted to Queens Hospital to heal an infection in her leg. At the hospital the discrimination against Margaret and her unwillingness to give in to it reached a high point.

Margaret had a single room. Though her leprosy was irrevocably arrested, other patients and even some staff members would hurry by her room for fear of catching the disease.

Every day at ten o'clock in the morning, a Filipino custodian on the hospital staff would quietly crack open Margaret's door, extend a long pole with a crudely attached broom and rack it unsteadily about Margaret's bed. She remembers, "he try hard to clean the room without ever coming inside. It no working. Worse. It make me angry."

After the first few days of fishing around the floor, dust and trash were accumulating in Margaret's room. One morning when the custodian's broom snaked in through the door, Margaret grabbed it and began to pull on it yelling, "Come in here and clean this place." The custodian pulled his makeshift pole one way. Margaret pulled it the other, all the time scolding, "Look under the bed. I think somebody die under there." Finally the duty nurse heard the commotion and rushed to intervene.

The next morning before the custodian came, Margaret pulled closed the curtains on her bed, pretending to be asleep. The poor unsuspecting little man took the opportunity to clean at least a wide circle around her bed. Margaret watched through the curtains as the circle narrowed. Then, just as the sweeper got within arms reach she swung the curtains out into his face and said, "Clean under the bed, not only just around it!"

"When the curtains hit that man in the face," Margaret tells, "he threw the broom down and ran for the head nurse crying." The head nurse chided Margaret for "torturing the poor fellow." But Margaret complained, "Why he nevah clean right, this buggah. I get my friends come visit. They say 'This one dump.' No clean evah."

Even after the nursing supervisor carefully explained to the custodian that Margaret's leprosy was arrested and that she was there with a noncontagious infection, the custodian only approached Margaret's bed at a distance and always with his back towards her, bent low over his broom. One day during Margaret's stay at Queens, she filled an empty spray bottle with water from her sink. At 10:00 A.M., the custodian backed into the room, stooped down over his broom and began to clean. Again Margaret feigned sleep. When the custodian reached his closest arc, Margaret threw open the curtains and pretended to sneeze. "Just when I pretend to sneeze," Margaret says, still laughing from the memory, "I spray his back side with that water! He know I give him leprosy for sure, and he run from that room screaming. I get one new janitor after that."

William groaned quietly on his bed. Margaret stood listening in the shadows. She saw a thin, old man lying there, but she was remembering her handsome, young father, his bare-armed muscles gleaming with sweat when he bounded up the stairs after work and swung her over the porch until she cried out with fear and delight. She remembered eating lunches with him in the parking lot of the Honolulu Iron Works when Moriah left them and William had to care for her out of the backseat of someone else's car; she remembered him drinking too much and beating her and snoring at the *ho'oponopono* and begging her to forgive him when he felt personally responsible for her leprosy; and she remembered him staring tearfully at her through the fence at Kalihi Receiving Station when he came to say "good-bye." She knew that soon they would be saying "good-bye" again.

"Baby?" he said quietly.

"Yes, papa. I here," she answered, going closer to him.

"Baby. Come." She leaned over the bed and took his hand. "You know papa going die," he said and before she could interrupt, he continued. "And when I die," he whispered fearfully, "I tink I going to *lua ahi* [the bad place]."

"How you know?" Margaret asked him.

"Because I no good," he said. How many times in those last weeks she had tried to explain that through Jesus' death and resurrection all could be forgiven. How many times he didn't understand. William struggled to breathe. Great drops of perspiration formed on his brow, ran down his chest and dampened the sheets.

"No forget *ke'a akua*," Margaret said, calling on an Hawaiian expression for Jesus, God on the cross.

"I don't know Him!" William answered.

Margaret started for the door. "I going bring the *kahuna pule* [the minister]. Not too late. Nevah too late."

William didn't answer.

Margaret remembers, "I pray for him so many times during those six months. I ask him to see one minister. Always he tell, 'Too late, Margaret. I bad.' He feel so guilty about what he do to me and to Ida and to the children. But when I try tell him that God forgive and all that, he say, 'Too late.' I say like Mother Alice say to me, 'No, nevah too late for God's forgiveness.' I show him words in the *Paipala* [Bible] that prove God is willing to forgive anybody anytime. But he no believe. Very sad when people no believe that God can forgive. 'Cause He can. I know." William died unbelieving.

Early the next morning, the ambulance came to take William's body away. Two young men tried to wheel it out the door on a four-wheel gurney, but they couldn't make it roll. The wheels seemed locked in place.

"Hard time," Margaret explains. "Hawaiian people, when they die, they no like leave. So my auntie whisper in the ear of William's body, 'No do that.' She say, 'Go in one good way. Nevah come back. Leave this house. Leave your daughter who take good care of you. Go now!' And just like that, the two boys push on the gurney and out it roll."

But the spirit of William came back to haunt Margaret, she remembers. "At night time he keep on coming back. I cannot sleep. I put lights on all night. I hear the walking of his feet. The groaning. So sad to die without forgive. I scared but finally, I say to him in Hawaiian, 'You know, I take good care you, Papa. I do good for you. How come you make like this? Coming here? Bothering us? You no ask God forgive. You no come *ho'oponopono*. You no make right. You sass all the time. You pride. Now you sad and no wondah. Go now. No come back.' And I cry and cry," Margaret recounts, "and after that, he nevah bother us again."

William's family sprinkled Hawaiian salt on the yard and throughout the house that very next day. According to Hawaiian custom, Hawaiian salt purifies a place and keeps the evil spirits from it.

Margaret locked the scarred door of William's tiny, rented bungalow. She had mopped and swept it clean of all her father's memories. His family and his friends were gone. Even his ghost had been exorcised by Margaret's desperate prayer. She took one last look around the place, then turned and walked down Kamoku Street past the Iolani School and through the public park.

Momentarily cut off by the Ala Wai Canal, Margaret sat on the same suitcase she had carried from Molokai to rest and get her bearings. Rowing crews practiced in their long, outrigger canoes. Retired executives and their wives barbecued on the balconies of their high-rise condominiums across the canal. A soccer game was in full play on the grassy field and across the Manoa Palolo Drainage Ditch, golfers laughed and cursed and kidded as they passed. Tourists jogged down Canal Boulevard in colorful matching jog-suits and young couples walked arm-in-arm along the water. No one spoke to Margaret. A young boy chased a badly kicked soccer ball that landed near her feet. For a second, he looked at her and though Margaret smiled up at him, he grabbed the ball and ran back across the field without speaking. She could feel the other boys staring and whispering, but she didn't look back.

Surrounded by people, Margaret felt terribly alone. She longed to return to Molokai and her friends at Kalaupapa. That "place of horror" had become her home, that "crowd of monsters," her dearest friends. They seemed so far away. She had no money. William's landlord didn't want Margaret in the house when he was trying to rent it to a new tenant. He didn't offer her the place, but she couldn't pay the rent anyway. Her hospital bill at Queens Hospital was already over $1200. No one would give her a job. There was no hope in even trying to look for work in her condition. And when she thought of welfare, she remembered standing in the long line to pick up William's check and feeling the stares and hearing the comments pointed in her direction.

The sun set prematurely behind the hotels of Waikiki. The afternoon turned cold. Margaret carried her suitcase in the shadows of those great resorts on sidewalks filled with tourists. She had no idea what drew her to this *haole* [foreign] place. A young surfer-type pedaled up beside her in the dusky darkness and asked, "Want a ride?" Then he noticed her crippled hands and feet and answered his own question. "No, I guess you don't." Quickly, he pulled away towards Kalakaua and the vacationers from Dubuque and Des Moines who could pay to ride behind him on his tricycle-rickshaw along the beach.

Margaret cut across the wide lawn of the Honolulu Zoo to the Waikiki Shell. The last Kodak Hula Show of the day was completing its grand finale. Margaret stood listening to those echoes from her past. Once more young men tapped out the ancient rhythms of the *kā'eke'eke* and once more, young girls draped in plumeria danced the ancient dance. Right foot in. Tap. Tap. Tap. Left foot in. Tap. Tap. Tap. Margaret remembered Iolani dancing with that little girl who had tripped and fallen, and she remembered Iolani's words: "When you fall, take only short time to cry. Then jump right up and dance again." This time Margaret did not feel like dancing. She picked up her suitcase and walked across the boulevard to the beach. The sun balanced on the horizon. A giant catamaran passed in silhouette loaded with tourists toasting Paradise. Then the sun lost its balance and fell into the sea.

Margaret sat in the darkness of the sands on Prince Kuhio Beach Park. For the first time in her more than fifty years of life, she didn't see any reason to go on living. Margaret rummaged in her suitcase. She found a large bottle of Bufferin, hobbled to the public drinking fountain and swallowed all the pills. Sometime in the hours before morning, a policeman found her, lying beside her suitcase in the sand, the empty Bufferin bottle clutched in her hand. When he couldn't awaken her, the officer called an ambulance which delivered Margaret, unconscious, to an emergency hospital nearby.

"Are you awake?"

Margaret heard the question coming from a terrible dream. She opened her eyes.

"You are awake! Good. You've slept all day. Look, I've saved you a bowl of soup from dinner."

Margaret let the cheery *haole* nurse brace her up against the pillows and feed her the hot bouillon drink.

"How come I stay here?" Margaret asked as she lay back on the bed.

"Because you took a lot of pills," the nurse answered. "But we flushed them right out of you and we'll have you good as new in no time."

Margaret rolled over on one side to escape the nurse's smiles. Out of the corner of her eye, Margaret could still see her bustling about the room, hanging the contents of her suitcase in the tiny closet and arranging the rest in a drawer or on a shelf.

"We'll make you 'comfy' here and get you back on your feet," continued the nurse. "Let's see now, where shall we place this lovely Hawaiian Bible? Why not here on the bedstand?" The nurse smiled again at Margaret and patted her. "Now, that's everything. Remember, your buzzer is beside you on the bed. The night nurse will come anytime you need her. 'Night, 'night," she called from the doorway. "Don't forget to say your prayers."

How many times Margaret had bustled about the hospital rooms of Kalaupapa's leprosy hospital, cheering up patients with a word or smile. Now, again, she was a patient in a hospital bed and those cheery words stuck in her throat. "Good as new." Margaret's chances of ever looking or feeling as "good as new" were long since lost in an endless cycle of chaulmoogra oil and carbon dioxide snow, injection needles and tracheotomy tubes. "Back on your feet." Margaret had no feet, only little stumps were left and those stumps had carried runny, infected sores for twenty years. "Say your prayers." Margaret had prayed and prayed and prayed. From that first *ho'oponopono* when she prayed with her family for healing from this awful disease to that last prayer for God to save Joe King before he died, her prayers seemed unanswered. And the Hawaiian Bible lying there beside her had been about the same as the medicine, a source of hope that never really worked to heal her.

"I feel sorry for myself," remembers Margaret. "I thinking that God nevah help me much. Since I was one small girl, I only come more sick. Nevah come well.

Everybody I love die. I wonder, 'where is God all that time?'"

Then in the semidarkness of her room, Margaret remembered when the old Hawaiian Bible was new. She was a lonely, frightened twelve-year-old again, in hula skirt and lei. As she stood in a room at the Receiving Station at Kalihi, Sarah Bunker rushed into her loneliness, that same Bible in her hands, and prayed a prayer that moved and comforted Margaret still. She remembered "Ma" Clinton, the iron-willed Kalihi Hospital administrator who helped the patients build themselves a church. Margaret recalled her last day in Kalihi, when Ma broke her own rules to hug her and to whisper, "God go with you, child."

That brief prayer had been answered. God had gone with Margaret to Molokai. Mother Mary Jolenta and the nuns were there, beginning and ending each day with hymns and prayers and readings from the Word, providing their young patients a home on that lonely isle. And Mother Alice was there, leading them in a nonstop celebration of life in the midst of all that death and dying. She taught Margaret how to water roses with her tears and then to give the flowers away.

All night, Margaret lay in her hospital bed remembering the people who had loved and helped her over those past forty years. They *were* God's people. He *had* heard her prayers. She had not been alone in Kalihi or on Molokai. God's people had been there with her every step of the way. Tears of gratitude and shame welled up and spilled over the old woman's wrinkled face. She would plant some roses here in Honolulu. She would not despair again.

Margaret walked past the auto parts store and the boarded-up chop-suey restaurant, down Lanakila Street, strewn with cars in various states of disrepair and stared up at the sixteen-floor Oahu Towers Project. She carried a small bag of groceries. Yesterday, she had waited for the elevator more than thirty minutes. Today she would walk up the nine floors to her little apartment in the west wing. Twelve hundred Hawaiians, Samoans, Filipinos, Vietnamese, Korean and Cambodian people lived there, crowded into rooms all around her. The halls stank of urine, beer and a strange mix of exotic, national aromas. The fire doors between the floors had been kicked in by vandals. Graffiti covered the walls with lurid text and graphic, mostly obscene, artwork. But it was now her home.

"We going walk?" Margaret's sister, Lani, one of Edith and Charles' eleven children, stood beside her and groaned the question, looking up at the tall building.

"*Ae*, we walk," answered Margaret, grateful that her sister had come to help her get settled into that box-like apartment so high above them.

For days, the two women had searched together for a home for Margaret. Each landlord they questioned found a different reason to keep the former leprosy patient from their building. The rental manager of the Oahu Towers Project had been no exception. However, after a noisy confrontation, Margaret and Lani found the building's social worker and told her their story. Jackie Wiggins turned out to be their first ally in the long and tiring search. She was a volunteer worker for the Susanna Wesley Community Center, serving the tenants in the building. When Margaret and Lani explained their plight, Mrs. Wiggins went to her phone and began to plead the women's case to the building's superintendent and finally to the supervisor of the entire government low-income housing project. Within hours, Margaret had the keys to an apartment on the ninth floor.

"Why on the ninth floor?" Lani wheezed as the two women climbed higher and higher in the building.

"Nice, the view up here," Margaret answered, knowing she didn't have any choice in the matter.

"You one stubborn *wahine* [woman], Margaret," her sister gasped. "Why you no stay with your daughter, Mary Ann? I bet she got one real nice place on the mainland."

"Because I like one place of my own," Margaret answered. She knew her children would be glad to have her. The tiny daughter who was taken from her and carried up over the *pali* so long ago lived on the mainland and had a family of her own now. One of Margaret's three sons was an Air Force officer with his own family on duty in Japan; another son was a United States Army officer with his own young army to raise; and the third son was a business man in Utah, separated from his wife, caring for two young children.

"Any of them would take me," said Margaret. "But I like be independent," she explained. "Living with them, I feel, you know, for a short while they will like you, yeah? But after that, maybe I get in their hair. I might scold the children. They no like I interfere. Moa better I stay right here. Besides, I going make friends here and if I leave, I going miss them."

"But how can you make enough money to live alone here?" her sister asked.

Margaret had it carefully figured. "I make plenty!" she answered.

"How much is plenty?" Lani demanded to know.

"I work thirty years as one nurse's aide on Molokai at Kalaupapa. Now they pay me $85 dollars pension every two weeks," Margaret explained.

"And how much is your bill at Queens Hospital right now?" Lani asked.

"Twelve hundred dollars," Margaret said, sheepishly.

"And how you going pay that bill when you nevah have no savings and no relatives that going die and leave you one pile?"

"I save five dollars every month. Slowly by slowly I going pay it off."

"Margaret," Lani reminded her sister, exasperated,

"you cannot live that long. They going trow you in jail."

The conversation slowed as the two women climbed the long, dark, cluttered stairway to the room above. As they turned into the corridor from the stairwell and walked the long, open balcony toward Margaret's apartment, a large coconut cannon-balled onto the walk in front of Margaret, bounced and rolled to her feet. Immediately, Margaret put down her grocery bag, picked up the coconut, leaned over the rail, and yelled at the balconies above, "O.K., who threw this?"

Above and hidden from her came the sound of young voices laughing and footsteps running away down the corridor.

Margaret dropped the unguided missile, picked up her bag, and walked on down the hallway, muttering, "Somebody going get killed in this place if not careful." Then, on impulse, she turned back, picked up the coconut, and put it into her grocery bag. "I save this. Maybe use it for protection."

Both women laughed. As Margaret fished in her pocketbook for the apartment key, Lani noticed a strange thing about another room down the hall.

"Hey, Margaret," she whispered. "Seem like one of your neighbors is *pupule* [crazy]."

Lani pointed at a nearby apartment with its windows entirely painted black from the inside.

"I think nobody live over there," Margaret said, as she forced open her own door with a quick blow of her shoulder when the key didn't work. "Nobody come. Nobody go. Must be empty."

As the two women entered Margaret's apartment, both squealed simultaneously. Inside the door were several bags of groceries, pieces of needed furniture, including an almost new recliner chair and an *"Aloha"* sign made of aluminum foil hanging across the little arch that divided the apartment into two rooms.

"Jackie Wiggins!" said Margaret, looking at the note on the drainboard.

"Oh, that Jackie is a wonder. She buy this muumuu I wearing now. When neighbors say, 'Leper, go away,' Jackie Wiggins tell, 'Never mind, Margaret.'"

Margaret lowered herself into the leatherette recliner. "And I know this recliner must be from Reverend Malcolm Turnbull. Nice. He is one counselor from Kailua. He works with Jackie. The doctor say I need to raise my feet. I went tell Reverend Turnbull. I thinking maybe he can get me one rope or something to hang them from the ceiling, but look at this beautiful chair!"

With the groceries stored, the new furniture in place and her sister safely on her way home, Margaret started down the stairs to 108 to thank Jackie Wiggins for the aid. As she passed those blackened windows up the open hall, Margaret peered in where the rather sloppy painter had missed a spot. The room inside was dark and trash was piled everywhere. She knocked on the door. No answer. Margaret knocked again.

"Go 'way," a squeaky male voice spoke from somewhere inside the darkened room.

"I no going away. Open up," answered Margaret.

There was silence a long time. Then the voice asked again, "Who dat?"

"I Margaret. I your neighbor. What's wrong with you anyway? You *pupule*, paint your windows black?"

No response. Finally, Margaret heard a key fumbling in the lock and the door cracked open. Margaret looked down on a middle-aged man. He was thin, bordering on gauntness. His clothes were dirty. The overwhelming smell rolled across the room and past him out the door. Margaret groaned.

"Phew! What a smell! This is one mess!" She pushed past the little man, gasped and backed out again.

"This place crawling with *'elelū* [cockroaches]. Too

many. How you can stand this place? How you can live here? What is your name?"

The barrage of questions flustered and embarrassed the man.

"Okada," he answered. "My name Okada. I like 'elelū. Dey my friends."

"O.K., Okada," Margaret said. "Tomorrow, I come back with one hammer and one bucket and we going kill a lot of your friends." She walked down the hall, shaking her head at the memory of literally hundreds of cockroaches crawling on the walls, on the ceiling, and on the floor.

Jackie Wiggins was in her office. She explained that Okada had been married to a 250-pound Hawaiian woman who, whenever she was drunk or angry, beat him senseless. Several months before Margaret moved into Oahu Towers Project, the woman had kidney failure and died. Now the man, his wits still damaged from his wife's mistreatment, feeling confused and lonely by her sudden death, had locked himself in. Margaret was the first person who had seen Okada in days. With 740 apartments in the building and no legal power to police them, Jackie's Susannah Wesley Community Center could only wait and hope for the best.

"No worry," assured Margaret. "I not waiting for nothing. Those 'elelū have one more night to live."

Early the next morning, Margaret knocked on Okada's door. When he didn't answer, she pushed the door open and found him sitting on the table staring at the cockroaches on the ceiling.

"We going clean up this dump now, Okada." He turned and looked at her.

"Whatsa matta wit you hands? Dey funny, like little hooks." He jumped down off the table and got down on his hands and knees, staring at Margaret's feet. "And you no moa toes, only little doorknob feets. Whatsa matta wit you?"

"Okada," Margaret said, threateningly, "my hands are

crooked. But they do lots of hard work. You get straight, healthy hands. But they are lazy."

With that, she handed him a bucket, got down on her knees and began to work. They spent the next four hours chasing and squashing and scraping up the little bugs that jumped and flew and flopped around the room.

"Nevah in my life I doing so much hard work like dis," Okada said, leaning against the wall and fanning himself with Margaret's bucket.

"That same afternoon," remembers Margaret, "Okada feel so good about his room that he go to the center, get paint and paint it one bright color. I fix curtains while he paint. End of day, I look inside the cupboard—no food; and in icebox. I tell, 'Come on, eat supper with me.' Next day, I get one food coupon and we buy plenty food for him with mine."

During those days Margaret spent helping her neighbor rebuild his apartment, she noticed that occasionally Okada would grimace painfully, turn his head to one side and hit his left ear with his left hand.

"What's a matter, Okada? You get water in your ear or something?"

"No," he always answered. "Long time get dis pain in ear. No wata. Long time nevah take one bath."

After several days of this, Margaret insisted they go to a medical clinic to have Okada's ear checked. She helped him wash and press his clothes. She found him a hat in the Community Center office. She got the exact change that it would take for the bus ride. When they were ready, the former leprosy patient from Molokai and the strange little man from 911 headed off to the free clinic at the Kaumakapili church. After a wait, Okada disappeared into the doctor's office and reappeared shortly, all smiles.

"Well," Margaret wondered, "what happen in there?"

"Noting," Okada replied. "Da docta went put da long pliers inside my ear and pull out one 'elelū. Den put inside da medicine. Feel O.K. now. Try. Look!"

Proudly, Okada held out to Margaret the body of a cockroach that had been living in his ear.

Margaret hurried down the last flight of stairs, across the cluttered yard of the Oahu Towers Project and into the front seat of Jackie Wiggins' little Toyota.

"Good morning, Margaret," Mrs. Wiggins called out, reaching across the front seat to push open the door for Margaret. "You look beautiful."

"I know," answered Margaret proudly. "Thank you." Margaret was wearing a new muumuu she had patched together from a remnant of cloth she discovered in the Center's "good-will" barrel.

"I so happy to go church today," said Margaret. "Since Kalaupapa, I stay lonely for church. Even if I no understand, I need go church."

"You're going to like Kalihi Union," assured Mrs. Wiggins, "and you will understand!"

Margaret rode in silence the few blocks to church, wondering not if she would like Kalihi Union Church, but if the people of that church would like her and accept her in spite of her handicaps. They walked across the parking lot and as they approached the rear entrance of the church, a woman about Margaret's age walked quickly across the narthex to greet them.

"Feel so good to be in church again," remembers Margaret. "We sing 'Savior, Like a Shepherd, Lead Us.' I remember all those people who went help me in Kalihi and on Molokai. I almost hear them singing beside me in the pew, you know. Sarah Bunker, "Ma" Clinton, Mother Jolenta, Reverend Alice, even Ida, all singing with me. And the people in the church no move away. They hand me the books. They smile. When came time for communion, the lady beside me went pass the bread. 'This is His body,' she said, 'Broken for you.' I said 'Thank you' and in my heart, I say, 'Thank you, Lord. Your body give me strength to keep my old body going.' Then Reverend Jay, he's the young minister, one Congressman's son, make us all hold hands for sing. That lady next to me she grab my hand and sing and sing. She was not afraid."

Mrs. Miller was the first to welcome Margaret. Others followed, after the service. The ministers, Stan Johnson and Jay Jarman, greeted Margaret warmly. Several young adults, Wayne and Sarah and Avis and Charlene, hung around after the service conversing with Margaret. During the weeks that followed, the church mobilized to help.

"I learn a lot from my church," remembers Margaret. "The people bring food for me. This rug is from the church; brand new, you know. Almost all what I own in my apartment is from the church. Everyone give. My curtains, both kinds, all given, pictures—everything. There was *aloha* in that church. There was something warm, you know?"

The gymnasium behind the Kalihi Union Church was overrun with an almost unbelievable mix of neighborhood people who lived in the shadow of the Oahu Towers Project. A carefree crowd of local youths, some in jeans and T-shirts, others—members of a Samoan church youth group—wearing their native lava-lavas, were playing volleyball.

In the gym lounge, a cluster of Japanese-American students from middle-class homes sat near another cluster of part-Hawaiian teens whose parents were laborers. Across the room sat a small group of recent Vietnamese refugees who had lost everything in their nation's civil war. Near them, was a group of *haole* kids whose parents were mostly military. This mixed bag of colors, races and languages had been drawn together by sports, music and fun. They all ate rice candy, shrimp chips and Oreo cookies and learned songs about a Jew from Palestine, written in Hollywood and recorded in Nashville, Tennessee. On the edge of this gym full of culture clash sat Margaret.

She didn't see any reason not to be there. She loved the

church and had decided to be there every time the doors were open. The Reverend Jay Jarman, Associate Minister at Kalihi Union, had developed a Thursday night "Liberty House" program in the gym as an experiment in Christian ministry and outreach to the neighborhood. After games and refreshments, there was music, a devotional message and conversation.

At that moment, however, poor Jay was trying to get the volleyball game stopped and to get the various cultural cliques together to participate in the evening's program.

Jay had just returned from a weekend preaching visit to Kanaana Hou, the Protestant church at Kalaupapa. When everyone gathered in the lounge, after a time of jokes and singing, he told them how the experience had affected him.

"At first," he confided, "I felt scared. I didn't even get close to them. I have kind of a weak stomach and a light head anyway. I could feel the old 'fainting fit' come over me whenever I focused in on a gnarled hand or a wasted face. In the cafeteria line, I saw patients stirring stew with wooden spoons clutched in what used to be hands, smiling at me with what used to be lips. Some of them had little red plastic tubes in their noses. Others were blind or had thick glasses and wispy hair drawn back and held together with rubber bands. In fact," he remembered, "their whole bodies looked like they were being held together with rubber bands and Band-Aids. This group of sufferers was cheerily serving up the food, and I wondered if I would get 'instant leprosy' if I put a bite of it in my mouth.

"I retreated to a corner," Jay told that mix of neighborhood kids, "where no patients were sitting and as I stared doubtingly down at my plate of food, one of the worst ambulatory cases at Kalaupapa came over and sat down beside me. He had no hand on his right arm, but inserted his wrist into the loop of a large, metal spoon and used that to push the food into a hole in the side of his face where his mouth and nose used to be. His whole face had just caved in so he simply shoved his food into the middle of that hungry hole. It was horrifying. I had to leave the room before I threw up.

"But little by little, my feelings toward the leprosy patients changed. I began to see them as people. Just before I preached on Sunday morning, a blind patient named Ben came up on his cane and, half-supporting himself and half-feeling his way along, asked to talk to the *kahu* [minister] who was preaching that day. I didn't shake hands with him, though he held out his ravaged hand to me. He knew I was standing there so he said quietly, "Please speak very slowly because I must remember everything you say." Later I learned that Ben loved the Bible but couldn't read it for himself. With his remarkable memory, Ben spent the entire next week, remembering the Word as I preached it. Thinking about it. Playing back my sermon in his memory, line by line. Praying about it. Thanking God for it. There was a quality of spiritual attentiveness about Ben I'll never forget.

"Then, the last night we had a *ho'olaule'a* [special music time]. The patients sang their Hawaiian ballads about the flowers or the waterfalls or the towns and villages of the different islands. They sang about Kona and Akaka Falls and Waimea on Kauai and "Lahaina luna." As they sang, I began to see them not as monsters, not even as leprosy victims, but as a community of different and very special people.

"At the airport, just before I left Kalaupapa, a gracious lady hobbled up with a seed lei that she had made for me during the night. They call the lei 'Job's tears,'" said Jay, holding up the lei for them to see. "She picked the tiny seeds off the bushes in her backyard and with her stumpy fingers sewed hundreds of seeds together to make the lei. She had not slept all night completing it. She was shy about giving it. She didn't want to offend me and kind of held it out at arm's length. I could tell she wanted to put it around my neck. So I swallowed hard and leaned down in front of her. It was my first physical contact with a leprosy patient. She smiled a big, broad smile and placed the lei around my neck. Would you believe," concluded Jay, "as that humble little lady stood beaming up at me, I leaned down again, kissed her on the cheek and hugged her? Something happened to me on Kalaupapa when I looked past their unsightly bodies and saw the beautiful people that lived inside."

Suddenly Jay stopped talking about his visit to the leprosarium on Molokai and turned to look at Margaret. All the eyes in that mixed crowd of young men and women focused on the interesting old lady in their midst. They had all seen her sitting on the sidelines, watching the volleyball game and listening to the music in the lounge. They had noticed her handicaps and walked in polite circles around her, guessing she might be a leprosy patient. In the silence, Jay smiled at Margaret and Margaret, embarrassed by the sudden attention, smiled and turned bashfully away.

"This is Margaret of Molokai," Jay finally continued. "You've seen her around the church over the past few months and tonight at Liberty House. She spent thirty-three years at Kalaupapa Leprosarium. Her feet are gone. Her hands are bent. Her body bears the scars of years of suffering and sadness, but she really is a beautiful person, isn't she?"

The kids looked at Margaret and back to Jay. A few nodded politely. Others just stared at the signs of Margaret's suffering.

"Let me tell you a story about Margaret," continued Jay. "When she first came to Kalihi Union several months ago, I thought she would be just another charity case, someone from the neighborhood that we could help. Instead, Margaret has helped me."

"Last Friday night," Jay recounted, "I had a meeting at the church that lasted till eleven o'clock and a six o'clock breakfast the next morning with only a few hours in between to catch some sleep. Rather than drive all the way out to our Pearl Ridge home, I planned to sleep at my office. So, I called Margaret to see if she would like to share a midnight snack from Diner's Drive-In. By the way," he interjected, "she likes two-scoop rice, macaroni salad and teriyaki beef!

"It's scary to visit that high-rise slum where she lives, even in broad daylight. I climbed the stairs fast, hoping no one would coconut me! You can't even read the walls there without getting embarrassed. The yo-yo latrines they call elevators are helpless, so I ran up the half-lit staircase, trusting that people would think the crazy *haole* was a pizza delivery man. I thought I'd make a quick pastoral call, eat and run. But Margaret had already fixed an old army cot with clean sheets and a comforter. 'No sleep on your desk, Jay,' she said. 'This moa betta.' It didn't take much for her to convince me to sleep there and wait for sunlight before running those stairs in reverse. So I stayed.

"After we pigged-out and talked for awhile, Margaret said, 'Jay, you so tired. Time for *moe* [sleep].' She turned the light down, came over to the cot and pulled the covers up under my chin. She tucked me in, patted my head, and began to sing to me. Picture it. I'm a grown man. I have kids of my own to tuck in. I grew up in suburban homes in Washington, D.C., and Oklahoma City. But here I am, lying on a mildewed army cot in a sky-scraping ghetto room, being tucked in by the tender hands of a leprosy patient who loves me and sings for me the old Hawaiian lullabies."

Suddenly Jay paused. "Margaret," he said directly to her, "my own mother is dead now. It's been a long time since she tucked me in or sang me to sleep. I felt such love from you the other night. I'll never forget it. *Māhalo!* [Thank you]."

At the end of the Liberty House meeting, after Jay had finished and the final benediction had been given, there was silence in the room. Nobody moved. Then, slowly, one by one, those neighbors from different worlds stood and moved toward Margaret. One by one, they greeted her. Some shook her hand. Others leaned over and kissed her cheek. Many blinked back tears. No one wanted to leave. The cliques of young people, separated from each other by their own private sufferings, became a caring circle around Margaret of Molokai. She had suffered, too. She would understand.

"It was very moving to see those college-age kids overcome their initial resistance to Margaret," Jay explained later. "They began to appreciate her with a genuine affection for who she is. In fact, since that Sunday, Margaret has had a whole fraternity of young adults from various cultures who are always dropping in to visit her at the Oahu Towers Project. They give her Christmas presents and birthday presents. They stop by with guitars to sing and play for her and the other people of the Project. They write little notes and cards to her and give her their school pictures. She has a whole photo gallery of young friends scotch-taped to the back of her apartment door. Those same young people that shied away from Margaret at first look, now take her places and show her off to their friends. Margaret is their heroine and their project and their joy, all at once."

Margaret heard a timid knock on her apartment front door.

"I coming," she answered loudly, placing one last tray of coconut cookies into her tiny oven and sliding a dozen half-burned cookies onto a paper plate.

"Why they always burn one side and no cook on the other?" she mumbled to herself.

Again she heard the knocking, this time much louder.

"I coming. Cool head, already. No rush." Margaret found her key and unlocked the door. Her half-blind friend, Cecilia, stood outside in the narrow hallway, near tears from anger and frustration.

"Come, Cecilia." Margaret took the woman by the elbow to lead her past the hallway clutter near her doorway.

"No," the older woman answered firmly. "I come for say good-bye."

Margaret stepped out onto the narrow, open walk. The Oahu Towers echoed with shouts and curses and raucous laughter. A gang of children careened down the nearby ninth-floor stairway and ran towards the two women. Another gang pursued the first. Margaret pushed Cecelia up against the wall to protect her from the bedlam before they both went sprawling.

"I going die," threatened Cecilia. "No can live in this place! I going seventeenth floor. Jump. This time for real, Margaret."

A string of illegal fireworks went off somewhere on the floors above them. Cecilia cringed, then pressed her hands tightly against her nearly sightless eyes.

Margaret reached out and took one elbow.

"O.K.," she said softly. "I help you."

Cecilia didn't move.

"Come," urged Margaret gently. "We go up seventeen." Margaret tried to lead her friend towards the elevator. Cecilia didn't budge.

"Long way, seventeen," Margaret teased gently. Still the old woman wouldn't move.

"Whatsa matta with you, Cecilia? You always trying to jump off this building but you nevah jump. Why not? You want to kill yourself, I help you."

Cecilia began to pout.

Margaret put her arm around her friend and led her into her own apartment. She put on the teapot to boil some water.

"You should be thankful, you know. You have brains. You went blind school. Kalaupapa blind people not like you. They nevah get any kin' school. But they no complain!"

She put a plate of coconut cookies in front of her friend and put Cecilia's hand on the cookies.

"Shame on you," said Margaret. "You no have to see all the dirty things in life. Like this building. Be glad you no can see. *Pilau.* Filthy. You would be too scared to live here. You going jump for sure then."

"You mad wit me, Margaret?" the woman asked.

"Yes, sure. I no like you talk like that. Foolish. Be thankful you not like me. I get leprosy and bad kidneys. One big hole inside my lung. Maybe cancer. I could die today but no time for that. Too much for do. Too many people for help. People worse off than us."

(Days after that confrontation, Margaret asked her doctor if she'd been cruel to Cecilia. The doctor said, "No. That is psychology. When you talk to them, they want pity. Pity will not help." "I use that psychology all the time now," says Margaret. "Psychology good for people, you know.")

When the two women finished their tea, Margaret took Cecilia to her apartment, washed and combed her hair, and helped her dress in a muumuu.

"Where we going, Margaret?" Cecilia wondered.

"Out to dinner," Margaret answered.

"How we going pay?" she asked. "How we going get there? They going let us in?" Questions tumbled out of the old woman.

"Too many questions nevah do nothing," Margaret concluded, and led her friend out the door.

Margaret and Cecilia took the bus. Inside Margaret's purse was the document that proved that her leprosy had been arrested and twenty dollars that she had saved from baking and selling cakes to her neighbors. Margaret spotted a large Chinese restaurant in the block near the next stop.

"You like Chinese food, Cecilia?" she asked, standing to get off the bus.

"No," answered Cecilia.

"Good," said Margaret, "then we eat Chinese food today. Come!" She helped her friend to the door, down the steps and up the sidewalk to the rather expensive-looking restaurant with two large pandas on a neon sign. As Margaret helped her blind friend through the door, the hostess hurried over and personally escorted them to a table in the shadows. Cecilia, comfortable in darkness, helped Margaret find the food. Margaret helped Cecilia eat it. The tragic-comic scene moved the manager and his staff. When the women left, he refused to accept Margaret's twenty dollars and invited them to come again as his guests.

"Every place I take Cecilia, like that," complains Margaret. "We no like eat free food. So we go to new restaurant every time. And every time same. No take our money. Nevah go back. No good for always eat free."

Twice a month Margaret takes Cecilia shopping. One week, they go out to eat. The next week, Margaret escorts her friend to the beauty shop. "She happy," says Margaret. "I take her on bus. I have hard time, but I take her. I find time. Many times I suppose to do something for myself. I give up my time for helping her. For helping others, too, yeah? That's why one of my friends said, 'You're always helping, but no time for yourself.' I tell, 'That's all right. I'm blessed you know.' I have all kind sickness in me and people say, 'How can you stay happy and active when you so sick?' I say, 'I make it my business to help them. Why stay home and cry?'"

"Margaret has become a human bridge between our Kalihi Union Church and the people in and around Oahu Towers Project," explains Reverend Jarman. "We have tried for years to reach the people there, but the place is really tough. When we joined other churches in Honolulu in a door-to-door campaign with bumper stickers, buttons on our Aloha shirts and a house-by-house canvass of the neighborhood, I volunteered for Oahu Towers. A big mistake! I took a college-age volunteer, Keith Matsumoto as my partner. He's about as brave as an ostrich, and I faint at the sight of blood. What a pair of cowards we were (with good reason). The first door we knocked on was flung open by a guy pointing a revolver at us. We both threw our hands up into the air, like in the old Western movies. Our questionnaires flew straight up and then floated down on us like a blizzard with very big flakes. 'Don't shoot, don't shoot!' I yelled. 'We're from the church.'

"We're lucky we got away. Later, Margaret found out the crazy guy we had surprised was fighting an inter-apartment war against another man two doors down who had stabbed him with a knife. He thought the culprit was 'messing with his lady.' That quick-draw cowboy wasn't too interested in us or our materials. But he knew Margaret. She lives just a few floors above him. The people in Oahu Towers Project see her hobbling up and down the stairs every day. She speaks their language. She shares their fears. She knows them and can work with them. We middle-class church-types are like visitors from another planet. Margaret lives where they live, and that makes all the difference."

For five years now, Margaret has shuffled up and down the corridors of the Oahu Towers Project sharing bones to make a pot of soup for a hungry family, counselling pregnant girls out of self-performed abortions or suicide, and lending cake money to people with overdue bills. Scolding some; listening quietly to others; praying for them all.

When Margaret found a Cambodian family suffering from the cold in a tiny room with cement floors, she asked the people of Kalihi Union Church for a carpet, and they delivered. When she found ten Samoans sleeping in one room without a mattress, she asked the church to cover the floor with mattresses. They did. Mrs. Eliza Ernestberg and a few others have backed Margaret with material goods, prayer and personal involvement. Now Kalihi Union has a part-time staff person working as Margaret's liaison. He coordinates the shipments of food and medicine, used furniture and clothing—all ordered up by Margaret.

"Those church folks are my bank," explains Margaret, "and I like God's banker out spending all their money."

"Everybody for one trip to Disneyland, say 'O.K.'"

Margaret was chairing the weekly meeting of the Hui Kukua Volunteer Club at the Oahu Towers Project. Around the room sat Okada, Cecilia, and almost a dozen other friends Margaret had enlisted to help meet the needs of their more than a thousand desperate neighbors. What the Kalihi Union Church provided, these volunteers distributed up and down the towers. They had decided to bring new life to that place and worked hard against difficult odds to do it.

"One, two, four, six, that's everybody," Margaret counted the unanimous vote. No one opposed the motion. Margaret believed her volunteers should be rewarded for their service, so she suggested this trip of a lifetime.

"That carries. Good! We going travel to Disneyland in California."

"But Margaret," a young Hawaiian girl, Linda, protested, "how we going raise enough money?"

"Margaret going make plenty cakes," interrupted Okada. "And I going sell them at parking lot."

Miraculously, John Okada had found a job as a parking lot attendant. He had developed a real skill at marketing

Margaret's homemade cakes to his regular customers. Of course he never told whose damaged hands had made those delicate pineapple-coconut creations.

"If we all work hard," Margaret answered. "We going make it. Good to dream big. Why not?"

Their decision made, the meeting of the Hui Kukua Volunteers dissolved in chaos. Everybody talked at once. Cecilia asked why she should work to go to Disneyland when she couldn't see it anyway. Okada jumped up and down with excitement. His entire life had been lived within blocks of that place. This would be his first time on an airplane, his first visit to the mainland. The new social worker, Janet Nakamura, smiled at the bedlam in the room. She imagined the impact on other visitors at Disneyland when Margaret of Molokai led her raggedy band up Main Street past Cinderella's Castle into the Big Bear Jamboree.

"Quiet!" yelled Margaret above the din. "We not through yet. We still get business. This not the Playboy Club, you know."

Suddenly she stopped mid-sentence and slumped to the floor in pain.

"Margaret!" Okada rushed to Margaret's side and rested her head on his knee.

"No worry, Okada," Margaret whispered, "I only get that same bad pain again." She tried to sit up, then grimaced and slumped back against Okada's leg.

Again, pandemonium broke out in the room. Janet ran to her office to telephone an ambulance. The Hui Kukua Volunteers stood around in shock and near hysteria. They knew Margaret was living on borrowed time. They knew her tired body might not fend off another illness. But they didn't know what they would do without her.

Margaret awakened twelve hours later in an intensive care unit of the Queens Hospital. She had undergone a five-hour emergency surgery for gall stones. Now she lay in bed "with needles and tubes stuck all ovah." She had grabbed up her Hawaiian Bible as they took her from her apartment and now lay reading it in the hospital room. Margaret remembers that the night nurse entered and found her reading.

"She say to me, 'Poor thing. I see you reading your Hawaiian Bible and the Lord doesn't answer you.'"

"I say, 'He does. He does. No talk about the Lord that way. Pain is His gift to me.'"

Apparently, Margaret put down her Bible, rolled back her covers and showed the nurse her damaged feet.

"Look, no toes; and my feet half-gone. Know why?" Margaret didn't pause for the nurse's reply. "My toes nevah drop off because of leprosy. I went burn them off in one campfire and I went cut them and make infection, 'cause I no feel. Leprosy kill my pain. Pain good. I like to have pain again. Keep you from hurting yourself."

"I know how leprosy works, Margaret," the nurse said, straightening Margaret's covers and rearranging the tubes Margaret's sudden demonstration had disturbed. "But your pain never stops. Your God is cruel to let you suffer so much. That's why I can't believe in Him."

The nurse looked down at the chart on Margaret's bed tracing her tragic medical history and felt sorry for the old woman in the bed. Margaret watched the healthy, young, *haole* nurse without a trace of suffering on her tanned, unlined face and felt sorry for the girl.

"God trust me with lots of pain." Margaret spoke quietly. "Pain is my blessing."

The young woman looked up incredulously at the woman ravaged by half a century of suffering.

"I no blame God for disease," explained Margaret. "I blame germs. Natural things, you know. But God come inside the natural things and give them purpose. I learn a lot from suffering. Now I stay tough. I'm not afraid. With God inside, I can live one good life in spite of suffering."

The nurse stared at the wrinkled, determined face, but said nothing.

"If my pain no get better," Margaret continued, "I become one better person from my pain."

Finally, the nurse spoke. "I wish I could believe like you, Margaret."

"Then believe," Margaret said. "Much harder to not believe, you know."

The old education building at the Kalihi Union Church was standing room only for the "Aloha Dinner" celebration. *Kahu* Jay was leaving Kalihi to begin a new ministry in Mililani Town. Members of the church had gathered to feast, fellowship, enjoy a program of entertainment and to say good-bye. Okada, now a proud usher in the church, led a long line of friends from the Oahu Towers to their special seats near the front. Margaret sat down nervously and waited for the program to begin.

She had weathered one more hospital stay, but was afraid she would not survive the next few hours. Jay had asked her if she would participate in the program and Margaret had hesitantly agreed. Now she was slowly dying of stage fright.

Jay leaned across the table to encourage her. Margaret scowled at him playfully then reached into her purse, pulled out a card and handed it to him. When the young minister opened the envelope, he found $100 in an assortment of bills and coins.

"For you, Jay. For your new ministry in Mililani."

Jay was amazed. "But, Margaret," he whispered, "what about your trip to Disneyland?"

"No worry. This for you. We make plenty more. One day we going Disneyland. Nevah mind."

The program began. Songs were sung. Prayers of gratitude and praise were prayed. Tributes were spoken. Then Jay stood to thank the congregation and introduce his friend.

"The psalmist David wrote in Psalm 150," he said,

"'Praise the Lord in his sanctuary. Praise him with timbrel and dance.' This will be a first for Kalihi Union and a very special gift to me. Forty-seven years ago a twelve-year-old girl was taken from a hula recital in the city hall to exile on the island of Molokai. Over those years, she lost three husbands to leprosy. Her four children were taken from her at birth and delivered to adoptive families on the mainland. Over the years, the disease mangled her feet and hands. She has suffered more than most of us can dream. She thought she would never dance again. But tonight, she agreed to stand before us and raise her hands to God and our church family. After years of struggle, Margaret will dance hula again—this time, a dance of praise.

"By the way," he concluded, "she made me promise to remind you that she is a leper and that she is afraid that she won't be graceful enough because of what the disease has done to her body. You know what they say of the hula, 'Keep your eyes on the hands.'? But tonight I say, 'Keep your eyes on her heart.'"

Jay sat down. The congregation applauded as Margaret walked up the short flight of stairs to the platform. She turned and faced the large assembly. Her friends from the Oahu Towers smiled up at her. One waved and giggled. Okada, wearing his bright, red carnation, beamed from the back of the hall.

In a quiet whisper-voice, Margaret said, "First I sing you a song. I no sing on key, but no matta."

Margaret fumbled in her pocket for the words to her song, words that she said God had given her after a late night conversation with the nurse at Queens Hospital. Then, trembling, she began to sing. At first her voice faltered, but then it grew in volume and in strength. The congregation strained to hear each word:

My Lord, I made this song for You.
To thank You for all what You done for me.

I know I cannot repay You,
So God, thank You so much.

In times of pain and in suffering
I turn to You for Your help.
You're always there to help me, Lord.
So Lord, thank You so much.

Praise God, from whom all blessings flow.
I thank You each day of my life.
So lead me in the way You want.
So, Lord, I thank You so much.

Then, slowly, Margaret lifted her arms and began to dance. Her movements were jerky and hesitant. She couldn't dance the graceful dance of childhood. She danced instead an old woman's dance of grace. In that warm, loving community at Kalihi Union Church, Margaret had found a family. No one would give her away this time. No one would abandon or abuse her in that place. The *hānai* child had come home to stay, and with every intricate movement, her entire body strained to thank God and His people for their work in her life.

The crowd smiled up at Margaret as she moved across the stage, her arms outstretched, her body swaying. No one shifted uneasily or felt embarrassed. No one laughed as she struggled to dance her dance of praise. There were tears of gratitude and tears of wonder shed that day. But there were no tears of pity, for Margaret's gnarled hands pointed up past the scarred creation to her Creator who gave her life and, in spite of sadness, strength to plant roses along the way.

RESOURCES

Books

Cooke, George P. *Kalaupapa*. Hawaiian Mission Society.

Damon, Ethel Moseley. *Siloama, The Church of the Healing Spring*. Honolulu: Hawaiian Board of Missions, 1948. (The original ledger describing the origins of the first Christian church built at the leprosarium on Kalaupapa, Molokai, "thoroughly fumigated is now kept in the vault of the Hawaiian Board of Missions in Honolulu," p. 9.)

Daws, Gavan. *Shoal of Time: The History of the Hawaiian Islands*. Honolulu: University Press of Hawaii, 1958.

Farrow, John. *Damien the Leper*. New York: Sheed and Ward, Inc., 1954.

Gutman, Jane. *Kahuna La'au Lapa'au*. An Island Heritage Book. 1979. (This authoritative book on the secrets and practice of Hawaiian herbal medicine has a helpful section describing the pre-Christian *ho'oponopono;* see pages 17–19.)

Handy, E. S. Craighill and Pukui, Mary Kawena. *The Polynesian Family System*. Rutland, Vermont: Charles E. Tuttle Company, 1958.

Martin, Betty. *Miracle at Carville*. Edited by Evelyn Wells. New York: Doubleday and Company, 1950.

Pukui, Mary Kawena and Elbert, Samuel H. *Hawaiian Dictionary*. Honolulu: University Press of Hawaii, 1957.

The New Testament in Hawaiian. New York: American Bible Society.

187

Yancey, Philip. *Where Is God When It Hurts?* Grand Rapids: Zondervan Co., 1977.

Pamphlets and Press

Brand, Paul W. *Escape from Pain,* a published lecture. Christian Medical Fellowship Publications, 157 Waterloo Road, London SE1 8XN.

Freedman, Marlene. *Molokai: The Friendly Isle.* Molokai Books, P.O. Box 263, Hoolehua, Molokai, Hawaii, 96729, 1977.

Hitch, Thomas K. *A New Look at Leprosy.* An original paper presented June, 1969, and published by the Health and Community Services Council of Hawaii, 96813.

Kawaiahao Church: The Westminster Abbey of Hawaii. A pamphlet used as a Visitor's Guide to a Registered National Historic Landmark, Honolulu, Hawaii. (Available through the Kawaiahao Church, King and Punchbowl Streets, Honolulu.)

Special Thanks to:

The Public Library of Honolulu for its excellent microfilm back-files of both the Honolulu *Advertiser* and Honolulu *Star Bulletin,* especially:

The articles describing Mother Alice Kahokuoluna's farewell service *(Star Bulletin,* 1/8/57, section 5, p. 1).

The article describing Mother Marianne's long service on the island *(Star Bulletin,* 8/2/41, Feature section, p. 1).

The Files and Pamphlets provided by the Hawaii State Health Department and the staff of the Communicable Disease Division.

Māhalo nui loa
The Reverend Jay Jarman

Māhalo!	Thanks!
Anwei Skinsnes	Lyla White
Mary Jarman	Erin and Michael White
The Reverend Gerald Chinan	Marjorie Smith
The Kalihi Union Church	Paul Brand, M.D.
Janet Nakamura	Margaret Brand, M.D.
Kevin Kunz, M.D.	Philip Yancey
The Reverend Dan Chun	Dr. and Mrs. John
Calvin and Florence Chun	Schmidt
Mark Kimura	Diana Trautwein
The patients and Staff, Hale Mohalu	Bill Youngblood
Hospital	Cindy Sittner
The Patients and Staff, Kalaupapa	Marguerite Shuster,
Leprosarium	Ph.D.
The Staff, Bishop Museum	Floyd Thatcher
The Staff, Honolulu Public Library	Ernie Owen
The Staff, Hawaiian Department of	Al Bryant
Health Communicable Disease	Beverly Phillips
Division	Jeanne C. Bryant
The Staff, Children's Missionary	
Museum	
The Staff, State Archives of Hawaii	
The Staff, Library, Honolulu	
Advertiser and *Star Bulletin*	